RECOVERING THE PAST
Celtic and Roman Mission

John Finney

DARTON·LONGMAN+TODD

First published in 1996 by
Darton, Longman and Todd Ltd
1 Spencer Court
140–142 Wandsworth High Street
London SW18 4JJ

ISBN 0–232–52083–6

A catalogue record for this book is available
from the British Library

Maps by Jeremy Dixon

Unless otherwise stated, quotations from the Bible
are taken from the Revised English Bible © 1989
Oxford and Cambridge University Presses.

Phototypeset by Intype London Ltd
Printed and bound in Great Britain by
Page Bros, Norwich

Contents

Preface   vii

Map: Great Britain   ix
Map: Europe   xi

Introduction   1

1 The Nations on the Move   9
2 Bede's *Ecclesiastical History*   16
3 The Evangelisation of England   21
4 The New Evangelism   34
5 The Monastery in Mission   50
6 Culture Clash   75
7 The King   90
8 Celt versus Roman   103
9 The Theology of Mission   116
10 The Seventh Century and God   132
11 Conclusion   140

Index   145

Preface

WHAT HAPPENED in AD 597 may seem merely of interest to historically minded mice who like burrowing through musty manuscripts. Surely the 'Conversion of England' is over and done with and of little contemporary significance? Two things make us think again.

The situation faced by those early missionaries is the same as that faced by us. As a result of their work, for the past 1,400 years England has been a 'Christian' country and the Church a foundation stone of society. Today, for the first time since the evangelists arrived, the situation is similar to the time before Augustine came. Christendom is fading fast and in another generation or two, if present trends continue, it will be no more than the Cheshire cat's grin. For the past 1,400 years the people of England knew what the Lord's Prayer was, and every child could tell the stories of the life of Jesus and knew that he died on the cross to save us. Now, once again, that is no longer true.

While this book deals with England, the phenomenon of a post-Christendom society is not confined to that country. It also applies to much of Western Europe, to Australasia and many parts of the United States and Canada. We can use the example of this small country to draw out lessons for a much wider geographical area just as a microscope which peers at a small area can show us details which we would otherwise miss.

Secondly, we have to face the fact that the 1,400 years of Western Christendom has been primarily Roman in character. The Church of Rome has dominated Western Europe. Even the Reformation was a movement within the parameters set by the Roman Catholic

Church. The decision to follow the Roman model in England is one that was taken at the Synod of Whitby in 664. Recently we have become more aware of another strand of Christian life, which, although owing allegiance to Rome, had a very different outlook and practice. The Celtic Church was both more traditional and more adventurous than the contemporary Roman Church. The riches of Celtic spirituality are only now becoming widely appreciated. However the Celtic saints were not only great people of prayer – they were also great evangelists and their methods and their approach to evangelism should be as important to us as their prayers. The fact that a good deal of the reality of the Celts has become hidden by later hagiographies and what I have called the modern 'Green Industry' should not blind us to the tremendous work which the Celtic Church did in evangelising England.

The Decade of Evangelism has woken up much of the Church to the perilous situation faced by all denominations. Fundamental questions have to be faced, and they are the same matters which faced Columba and Augustine and Aidan and Paulinus.

How can we bring the gospel to contemporary society?
How can we help them to hear it?
What shape of church is appropriate for them?

Watching the men and women of old answering these questions can help us to realise the importance of the questions, and learn from their responses, whether or not we adopt them for ourselves.

In this book I argue that evangelism in England has changed remarkably, even over the five years since the start of the Decade: this 'New Evangelism' has begun to answer some of the questions which the early evangelists encountered, and it is interesting to note that their solutions are in many cases the same as ours. Even more significant is the fact that 'New Evangelism' tends to have a Celtic rather than a 'Roman' slant.

This is what we are going to explore.

RECOVERING THE PAST

Iona

STRATHCLYDE

Bamburgh • Lindisfarne
Old Yeavering •
BERNICIA

NORTHUMBRIA

Jarrow
Roman Wall Monkwearmouth

Withorn

Armagh • Bangor

Bradbury
Whitby
Lastingham
Rievaulx

Ripon • DEIRA
York •

Dewsbury • River Humber

Caister

Kells •
Dublin •

Chester •
Bangor

Lincoln •

Lichfield •

EAST
ANGLIA

MERCIA

Dunwich

Wexford •

HWICCE
Gloucester •

Hertford
St Albans •

Colchester •
Sutton Hoo

Caerleon •
Dorchester • River Thames
London
Tilbury

Thanet

Llantwit Major •

Bath •

Rochester •
Canterbury •
KENT

WEST SAXONS Winchester •

RECOVERING THE PAST

Introduction

The end of Christendom

The New Agers have got one thing right. Spiritually this country *is* moving into a new age. We do not have to agree with their beliefs about the Age of Aquarius to know that Christendom, as an overarching cohesive body of belief and morals held to by the great majority of people in the 'West', is evaporating. No longer does nearly everyone know the Parable of the Sower, or think that self-sacrifice is something to be admired. The legalistic discussion about disestablishment and the coronation oath, and whether the monarch is 'Supreme Governor of the Church of England' is merely a symptom. At the end of the millennium we are rightly questioning this inheritance of Christendom, and asking if a new age needs new patterns of working. It would be surprising if no change was needed.

Today, as in the first century, Christ is jostled in the market-place by many other gods. The old gods of materialism and greed are still there, but other, more earnest newcomers are also setting out their stalls: the great world religions such as Islam and Hinduism, over 1,600 large and small 'New Religious Movements', are all shouting 'Come and buy'. The Christian Church can be made to look like an amateurish Women's Institute stall alongside the modern glitz of a hypermarket – even though its wares may be more wholesome.

One great former counterpoint to Christianity also looks threadbare: politics no longer sets out utopias or claims to make all things well. The post-communist, post-Thatcherite world is curiously bloodless. Few join political organisations and even fewer go to party meetings. A new politician may stir some interest but after a while he or she looks as tarnished as the rest – a Ross Perot in the United States or a Silvio Berlusconi in Italy promise much but deliver little.

A distaste for party politics has turned the attention of many to 'issues' – particular viewpoints about a single cluster of ideas: ecology, extra-terrestrial encounters, feminism, vegetarianism, political correctness, animal rights. Decent or dotty, they claim people's allegiance and energy, but for only a few are they a passion. If they lack the undergirding of a religious base they can become a substitute for faith rather than the outcome of faith, and become intolerant of other viewpoints and careless of the means they use to make their point.

We must not overpaint the picture – there are still vestiges of Christendom. The 'rites of passage' still attract many: people bring their babies to be 'done'; they see marriage as having a more than secular importance; most want to have Christian burial. But the trend of the figures is clear. If there is no revival of faith, the last vestiges of Christendom will disappear in a few generations and the Christian Church will consist only of those who have deliberately chosen to follow Christ.

Christendom has lasted for 1,400 years. The last time when the spiritual life of England was up for grabs was at the time of the seventh-century 'conversion', as historians call it. Since then England has had Christian roots.

The beginning of Christendom

In AD 597 two symbolic events took place. The Celtic St Columba died at Lindisfarne and the Roman St Augustine came to Canterbury. That period was the last when Christian evangelists in England were faced by a mostly non-Christian population. Only in this generation can preachers feel at one with those who entered an Anglo-Saxon village and encountered the pagan teachers, and stood in the market-place preaching the word amid the jeers of the inhabitants. The Decade of Evangelism has brought the issue of mission to the unchurched to the forefront. How did our forefathers in the faith (and 'foremothers', because there were some doughty women involved) deal with a pagan society? The Celtic methods of evangelism were different from the Roman model which Augustine brought to Canterbury. Are there things from which we can learn?

Today is a religious age. In the supermarket of religions people pick what they like from the shelves – some may collect a fundamentalism which gives a tight structure to their lives, others a 'touchy-feely' self-development package, others a cult which 'love bombs' them into a deeper sense of community than they have ever experienced before. It may not satisfy. The Roman world of the third century had a similar proliferation of alternatives: 'There were too many cults, too many mysteries, too many philosophies of life to choose from. You could pile one religious insurance on another and still not feel safe.'[1] The young Augustine of Hippo described the Rome of the fourth century: 'In public we were cock-sure, in private we were superstitious, and everywhere void and empty.'

There is interest in religious experience. 'Spirituality' is a growth industry. Within Christianity the Charismatic movement, Taizé, and the influence of Iona, Focolare and Cursillo, all point to an interest in a direct personal experience of God.

Nowhere is this more true than in Celtic spirituality. It seems to strike chords with the twentieth century in a way which is not true of more traditional Latin models.

> It does seem to speak with almost uncanny relevance to many of the concerns of our present age. It was environment friendly, embracing positive attitudes to nature and constantly celebrating the goodness of God's creation. It was non-hierarchical and non-sexist . . . it seems to speak with a primitive innocence and directness which has much appeal in our tired and cynical age.[2]

But we shall need to look at this more carefully – is this a reading back of modern yearnings into a far distant twilight, or was it factually true?

The 'Green Industry'

Is there a 'Green Industry' which is projecting into the grey Celtic mist our own desires, with little or no basis in historical fact? We have to admit that there is something about the Celts which addles the mind and leads to preposterous claims and foolish assertions.

Some see Celtic Christianity and the druidic religion which preceded it as politically correct, ecologically conscious and all-tolerant. The two faiths (for they are closely related in many people's minds) are seen as providing a faith for the future in the way that the weary colossi of Catholicism and Protestantism manifestly fail to do.

Not only is this historically inaccurate, but it does less than justice to the remarkable exploits of the Celtic churches, and the undoubted contribution their thinking can make to modern Christianity. The Celtic saints did not wander around making poems about nature, but proclaimed the faith with a fair amount of cursing of evil thrown in and with an intensity which we find almost too emotional. They believed in the miraculous and in an interventionist God. They prayed for hours in agonising positions and, far from respecting their bodies created by God, subjected them to disciplines which seem brutal to us. They believed in condemnation: Patrick excommunicated the soldiers of Coroticus as 'rebels against Christ'. The monk who received the sacrament 'although he has sinned shall do penance for a hundred days on bread and water'.

Nor is the druidic religion from which they had been converted much different. The historical truth is that we know very little of druidism in Ireland in the fourth and fifth centuries; if we know all too little of Christianity which has written records, how much less about an earlier illiterate Ireland that was just emerging from the Iron Age. As Alannah Hopkin says of the pre-Christian religion,

> There are suggestions of sun-worship and a great reverence for the dead, There were many sacred rivers, streams and wells ... They held certain gods in awe – Lig and Dagda for example – but we know virtually nothing about how they worshipped them, if at all ... the main impression we have of the religion of pagan Ireland is one of animism dominated by superstition.[3]

It is strange how so many people today make Celtic Christianity into a focus for their own longings. It is claimed that the Celts had a healthier view of sex, that women were equal with men, that they had a creation-centred rather than a salvation-centred faith, that they had a non-dogmatic, *laissez faire* Christianity open to new thinking, that they worshipped with joy and laughter. These are half truths and dangerous with it. We do not honour the Irish saints by making them projections of ourselves. Their achievement is remarkable, and their legacy all too little known until recently, for much of it was locked in the Celtic languages. We are best to see them as they were – men and women of their age.

The people of God

Ecclesiological questions abound today. What is the place of the bishop? what is the right way to organise a church? what is the right relationship between clergy and laity? Parish boundaries, establishment, the freehold and patronage are all part of the legacy of Augustine (and, particularly, of his successor Theodore). It was this period which established the relationship between the priest and the laity – and the local landowner. For the established church the Reformation did little to alter this, for it did no more than it set out to do – reform a basically Roman pattern. Few, except the Congregationalists, the Anabaptists and more extreme sects, looked more deeply – and were mightily persecuted for it.

The Celtic churches were far less hierarchical and bishops were just people doing a certain job – not those at the top of the heap. Bishop Michael Marshall has been reminding us the colour for the episcopate in the early Church was the green of growth, not the purple of imperial majesty. It has to be said that attempts to avoid hierarchy have been generally unsuccessful in western churches: it is frightening how quickly the New Churches have evolved the equivalents of bishops, priests and deacons. Is this inevitable? Can we learn from the contrasts between the Celts and the Romans?

Holiness

Although we live in a church which too seldom uses the term, holiness is attractive. Aidan and Cuthbert and Ninian and the rest were holy men. Prayer was central to their lives: they longed to be with God. When Cuthbert found that people interrupted his prayer he went to live on an island; when people got boats and visited him he found an island that was more remote, yet still people came, including kings and bishops; eventually he was persuaded to become a bishop himself and in the two years before his death profoundly affected half of Northumbria. Even the most Protestant has to be moved by the relics of Cuthbert in the Treasury in Durham Cathedral. We need to look also at the influence of the 'holy place' – to this day Iona, Lindisfarne, Jarrow have an indefinable something about them.

Their spirituality was that of those on the edge. They were groupings of Christians clinging onto faith at the edge of the known world. Many of them had been pushed from their homelands in what we now know as England – some even fled from France. It is a spirituality and theology of the insecure – and we know now that sounds different from that produced by the successful. It was a faith of those who knew more suffering than happiness in this life. Bede wrote only two and a half miles from Wallsend – the 59-mile wall which was seen as the boundary between Roman civilisation and barbarism. He was 1,500 miles from Rome – a journey which could well take a year or more.

We have to be careful. There can be more than a touch of being a romantic little Englander (or Welshman, or Scotsman or Irishman) in this interest in all things Celtic. Antiquarianism can be comforting – we can explore the riches of the past without being troubled with foreigners. In particular we have to avoid being prejudiced against the Augustinian mission on the grounds that it was a group of Italian monks from Rome. The Celtic saints were not bulldog Protestant British with a touch of the Charismatic. We must avoid awarding people white hats and black hats. As Henry Mayr-Harting, a recent historian of the period writes, 'I am aware that the whole Roman–Irish dualism ... is an over-simplification' – though it has to be said that he makes much of it in his book.[4] It is a much more tangled, and fascinating story than that. Both Celts and Romans looked to the Pope as the fount of authority – that was the kernel of the argument at the Synod of Whitby in 664. Nor did they preach different gospels from each other – though they may have contextualised it differently and had different emphases. Nor must we assume that we have to copy everything Celtic – Rome and the western tradition has much that is valuable above rubies. Rome and Ireland both represent primary creative forces – in some ways distinct, although their similarities were more significant than their differences. It is more akin to the growing influence of the African, the South American and the South East Asian churches today – creative forces whose fullness we can only begin to guess at. They have the same Scriptures and the same faith as western churches, but the way in which they express these in their own context leads to a burgeoning of creativity which can make us seem unspiritual, effete and querulous.

This is particularly important, because in this book I shall suggest that we may need to reinterpret the popular history of the Conversion – and be cautious in our use of that great historian Bede, who is our primary authority. As William Chaney warns us, 'The Romanist interpretation of Anglo-Saxon England has held sway in so many areas that its Germanic past has too often been seen through Mediterranean eyes.'[5]

Nomenclature

Some preliminaries about names. They can be confusing, for the Scotti were Irish and some Irish came from Gaul, and Northumbria included a good deal of present-day Scotland.

The *British* were the remnants of the inhabitants who had been pushed westwards by the Anglo-Saxon invaders. They now lived in Wales, Cornwall and parts of Lancashire and abroad in Brittany and elsewhere.

The *English* refers to the newly arrived Anglo-Saxons who came to inhabit what is roughly England today.

The *Irish* refers to the people of Ireland, and also those of Irish roots who came into England via Scotland and Gaul and Wales.

The *Welsh* lived where they do today.

Preliminaries

By 597 the British Isles had had Christians around for at least four hundred years. Tertullian, wrote *c.* 210 of 'regions of the Britons inaccessible to the Romans but subject to Christ': even by then the Celts were touched by the faith, for he must have been referring to Ireland or Scotland which were beyond the outskirts of the Empire.

By the early fourth century there were bishops – more incidentally than the three who famously couldn't pay their way to Rome and plaintively appealed for help (some readers may have had similar letters from two-thirds world bishops). By the time the Anglo-Saxons arrived there were churches and congregations up and down the land. But there was a fatal weakness – the faith was mainly urban and mainly upper-class.

Then came the Anglo-Saxon invasions. By the time Augustine landed in 597 the main Anglo-Saxon kingdoms had been established and the process of absorbing the minor kingdoms was beginning: it ended with present-day England divided into three – Wessex, Mercia and Northumbria.

The British were pressed back or absorbed until the church remained strong only in Wales, Scotland and Cornwall. Even then they were under pressure – Gildas the Welsh monk in 540 spoke of the time of tribulation when the Anglo-Saxons pressed almost to the western sea. Significantly, when Augustine wanted to meet the leaders of the British church, they came from the west to the river Severn and he came from the east. It was thought that the British Christians did not evangelise the Anglo-Saxon, for as Bede says with scorn: 'Among other unspeakable crimes . . . they did not preach the faith to the Saxons who dwelt among them'.[6] They became marginalised in spiritual as well as geographical terms. Even the British language was replaced by Anglo-Saxon. They were no longer near the centres of power. Christianity seems to have virtually disappeared. The scene in Canterbury when Augustine arrived is a parable – he found a church there, but it was in ruins.

Notes

1   E. R. Dodds, *Pagan and Christian in an Age of Anxiety* (1965).
2   Ian Bradley, *The Celtic Way* (1993).
3   *The Living Legend of St Patrick.*
4   *The Coming of Christianity to Anglo-Saxon England* (3rd edn, 1991).
5   *The Cult of Kingship in Anglo-Saxon England* (1970).
6   Bede, *Ecclesiastical History* 1.22.

Chapter 1

The Nations on the Move

The coming of the Anglo-Saxon

THEY CAME in boats. If they were rowing they could make three knots. But they were sensible sailors and the wind could push their speed up to nine or ten knots. The journey from Denmark or north Holland might take a week, possibly only a couple of days given good weather.

When they came to fight there were about 50 fighting men on board but when they came to settle there would have been 20–30 people with their baggage. A leader might have two or three ships under him. It was not a day of big battalions. A seventh-century law code describes a group of 7 men as thieves, 7–35 became a band: more than 35 was an army.[1]

They spoke to each other in a Germanic language, but significantly it had picked up some Latin words. They lived beyond the boundary of the Roman empire, but it could be crossed, and they were familiar with Latin speakers and traded with them, so that trinkets from the Mediterranean world are found in their graves.

It is curious to reflect that from this tribal language of the northwest lowlands of Europe sprang the global lingua franca of today, for English is spoken by more people than any other language in history.

Why did they come?

In part they were *political immigrants*. From far away in the east the Huns had come on like an evil storm until Attila burst into Gaul and nearly reached the Channel coast. But that was the furthest reach of the furthest wave. In 454 he was defeated and the Huns retreated to the Rhine and were then forced to withdraw still further east. But the knock-on effect had devastated the Roman Empire. Their early advances had pushed the Goths over the border in present-day Romania and they had settled in the Balkans, menacingly close to Rome. Alaric the Goth sacked it in 410.

We still speak of *Gothic* horror films, of *hunnish* behaviour, of *vandalism*. Their names have menace even today. To contemporaries the threat was all too real: one Christian evangelist near the Euphrates was told to 'try cursing the Huns, who are said to be coming and wrecking all Creation'.[2] To the Angles and the Saxons and the Jutes the terrible hordes might be just over the eastern horizon. They looked over their shoulder as they set off for Britain for the Huns had set all of Europe on the move and other tribes pressed on their lands.

But they were *economic immigrants* as well. Life was harder. The climate was getting worse and the sea level was rising. Summers were shorter, winters colder, storms inundated more and more of their low-lying agricultural land. Britain seemed more settled, more able to bear them.

There was a third reason – in some areas *they were invited* into England. In its later years the Empire had welcomed barbarian tribes over the border provided they acted as guards against other barbarians. In Kent Vortigern brought in Anglo-Saxon allies to help to defend his kingdom. History showed that it was not a wise thing to do.

Whether pushed or invited or in search of a better life they came. Julius Caesar conquered Britain with 40,000, William of Normandy brought 8,000 in 1066. The Germanic tribes of Angles, Saxons and Jutes came a few score at a time – and the evidence suggests that they conquered more thoroughly than the more highly organised invasion fleets of the Romans and the Normans.

The decay of Rome

Alone in the Empire the first part of the fourth century had been a prosperous time for the province of Britannia. Towns grew, villas were extended. The population was at a peak not reached again for 1,400 years. 'Barbarian' pirates occasionally raided the eastern and southern coasts and an extensive system of lookouts and strongpoints had been established, but for most life was settled and good. The troubles of the Empire did not impinge on them.

It could not last. In the second half of the fourth century a period of slow decay began. Few new villages were established, trade diminished, life moved out of the towns to the countryside.

As the pressures on the centre of the Empire mounted, the Roman troops began to be thinned out. Sometimes they returned to Rome with a military leader in order to challenge for the emperorship, as with Constantine; sometimes they were recalled by a harassed senior officer. They were not replaced. The final realisation that they were on their own seems to have dawned on the native British about the beginning of the fifth century. In 410 Honorius told them to look after themselves. In 446 they made an appeal for help to Aetius in Gaul but the conqueror of Attila refused.

Some pattern of Roman city life remained. St Albans was putting up new buildings in about 450 and further west Caerwent, Gloucester and Cirencester had a semi-Roman lifestyle until the following century. But the pleasant Roman urban life with its handsome buildings and its baths and theatres and civilised conversation was petering out. Trade was only a fraction of the bustle of previous years, and money became worthless: the merchants could not operate.[3] The steam had gone out of the engine and it was slowing down leaving only the remembrance of greatness. But as we shall see, this memory was more enduring than the exasperation of the British at a toothless Rome which could not protect them.

The Germanic tribes had come to raid. When the power of Rome waned they stayed to settle: up the rivers of the south and east they penetrated and established their encampments. From these they pushed inland. The fear they conjured is like that provoked by their Viking successors four centuries later. The historian Orosius writing around 418 described them as 'the Saxons, a tribe living on the shores of the Ocean in inaccessible swamps and dreaded for their bravery and rapidity of movement'.[4] Gildas, a century later, just calls them 'wolves' (*ferocissimi Saxones*).

They did not find it easy. It took decades to conquer the land. In Sussex, Aelle with three shiploads of settlers landed in 477. It took them fourteen years to work the fifty miles along the coast to take Anderida (Pevensey) 'and slew all that were therein'. They penetrated hardly at all inland, leaving the Celtic fields on the downs untilled. Cerdic landed with five ships near Southampton in 495, but it took twenty years to secure even the immediate area. The invasions were small scale, uncoordinated, as unlike D-Day as can be imagined: a few ships slipping into the harbour, local skirmishes, a handful of newly dug graves.

After the departure of the legions the British had separated into small areas under warlords. A few were able to gather a group of allies by force of personality or military prowess. Leaders like Ambrosianus Aurelianus and the semi-legendary Arthur defended the land. At Mons Badonicus (c. 500) the Anglo-Saxons were so routed in a major battle that some of them even returned to the Continent. There was a lull: when the excitable monk Gildas was writing in about 540 he remembered a time when the invaders had almost reached the Irish Sea, but now much of the country was at peace, though great swathes of the east were occupied.

He spoke too soon. Towards the middle of the sixth century the Anglo-Saxons began a further push westwards. Bath was occupied after the battle of Deorham in 577. In the north the fortress of Bamburgh was occupied in 547, though it was a further fifty years before they could break out of the enclave around it. By 600 the main Anglo-Saxon kingdoms had been established. Northumbria occupied east of the Pennines from Humber to the Tweed and soon enlarged this to include Lancashire, Cumbria and South West Scotland. In the south there was Wessex and in the Midlands Mercia. On the circumference there were lesser kingdoms which enjoyed or endured different degrees of dependency and occasionally made a bid for independence.

They were not like a modern kingdom – they were a confederation of tribes ruled over by a king who exacted tribute from the lesser rulers. The king 'was the leader of his people rather than the ruler of a state ... he was not King of Northumbria but "King of the Northumbrians". He did not have a fixed capital but travelled between a number of royal residences, at Yeavering, Bamburgh, York and others.'[5]

What happened to the displaced Britons is a major historical conundrum. In the areas controlled by the Anglo-Saxons they seem to have totally disappeared. The Anglo-Saxon language adopted barely a dozen British words;[6] their place names are Germanic rather than British (except in Cornwall). Only in the South West are there any number of British cemeteries. The Roman cities were abandoned as places to live. The invaders seem to have subjected the British to ethnic cleansing.

On the face of it this is improbable. Captured peoples make good slaves to till the land and do the menial jobs. They can even be traded at a profit. In such a piecemeal occupation surely the fens and forest which covered so much of the countryside must have hidden scattered remnants of the defeated peoples.[7]

But the evidence for coexistence is just not there and in the absence of new discoveries it has to be accepted. The British seem to have been either expelled or exterminated. Historians have always found this hard to accept: Richard Hodges says of the Anglo-Saxon settlement of the Winchester area in the early fifth century, 'presumably the two communities integrated without rancour' – it sounds like common sense, but there is little evidence for the statement.[8] Nora Chadwick said in her O'Donnell lecture, 'I firmly believe myself that the predominant element in the population [of England] is Celtic. I am aware that proof is not possible.' But this seems to be highly unlikely – what evidence there is suggests that the native British seem to have been almost entirely dispersed, and with them the Christian faith, except in some of the western areas.

Some of the British escaped. Westwards the refugees fled into Wales and the far South West. Northwards they moved into Scotland. Southwards they sailed to Brittany and gave it its name as early as the 460s. By the 570s there was even a large enough British contingent in northern Spain to warrant a bishop of their own.[9] Brittenburg in the Rhineland and the several French villages called Bretteville point to other settlements.

The move from the Continent had been a good one for the Anglo-Saxons. During the fifth century they had buried their dead with a few trinkets; in the sixth century precious swords and necklaces accompanied them to the afterlife. By the seventh century the splendour of Sutton Hoo was possible: a king was buried in a great ship with treasures which came from the four corners of Europe.

The other tribes

Not only the Anglo-Saxons were on the move in the fifth and sixth centuries. Less well documented and less well researched are the movements in the Celtic world between Ireland, Scotland, Wales and beyond.

Wales received considerable immigration, along with the Dyfed dynasty, from Ireland. Cunedda and his people came from the lowlands of Scotland to found a long lived dynasty in North Wales. Along with the advent of the British refugees, it was a time of turbulence and trouble in Wales, with people displaced and much wandering.

The Picts still occupied the North and East of Scotland, but invaders from northern Ireland occupied the South West to form the kingdom of Dalriada. The invasion led to intermittent warfare between the Irish and the Picts for over 300 years until they were united under Kenneth MacAlpin in about AD 850.[10]

For the Irish it was a time of expansion, as they went beyond Wales and Scotland to Cornwall and Brittany, and some of them, as we shall see, to the furthest reaches of Europe.

The movement of shadowy peoples under half-forgotten kings is important in deciphering the stories which lie behind the apparently well known. Aidan, Columba, Augustine, Paulinus – these are names we know. But they often moved with their people, and the language they spoke, the methods they used and the impact they made was often determined by their background. In particular the Irish achievement had a lasting impact on the English church.

Notes

1 P. H. Blair, *The World of Bede* (1990).
2 The story of Symeon, who gave the youngsters of the village a haircut, is recounted in Robin Lane Fox, *Pagans and Christians* (1986) pp. 289ff.
3 Money had been used for over 300 years for trade and paying tax, much of it coming into Britain as soldiers' pay. It ceased to have value about 425 and no money circulated until the Anglo-Saxon kings issued coins in the late seventh century. This is one reason why so many coin hoards from this period have been unearthed – if your money has ceased to be of value you hide it in the hope of better times.
4 *Seven Books against the Pagans.*
5 Ann Reid, *Church–State Relationships in the Seventh Century* (n.d.). When

examining the evangelisation of England and even the theology of the preachers the position of the king is of the greatest importance; it is looked at in more detail in Chapter 7.

6 In contrast, French adopted 500 Celtic words.

7 A seventh-century hermit in search of solitude complained of being disturbed by British tribespeople in the depths of the fenlands of East Anglia, but that is the only hint of survival.

8 *The Making of Britain: The Dark Ages* (1984). Some historians feel there is a hidden racism observable in those writers who try to make the evidence show that there was so much intermingling that there is only one nation in these islands: cf. Peter Berresford Ellis in *Celt and Saxon* (1993).

9 James Campbell, *The Anglo-Saxons* (1991). It is possible that the British in Spain came as settlers from Ireland rather than as refugees from England.

10 The invading Irish from the Antrim area were called Scotti and gave their name to the nation.

Chapter 2

Bede's *Ecclesiastical History*

IT IS impossible to write about the evangelisation of England in the seventh century without forming a view about Bede's *Ecclesiastical History*.

The book is an extraordinary achievement, far more judicious and comprehensive than anything produced in Europe at the time or for long afterwards. There has never been a period when it has been disregarded. King Alfred had it translated into Old English. It was one of the first books to be printed in England (in 1475). At the time of the Reformation it was regarded as strongly pro-Roman and was recommended Catholic reading – indeed the first translation into modern English was made by John Laet in 1565. He sent a copy to Elizabeth I with a covering letter in which he underlined this: 'Your Highness shall see in how many and weighty points the pretended reformers of the church in your Grace's dominions have departed from the pattern of that sound and catholick faith first planted among Englishmen by holy St Augustine our Apostle.' Wisely he sent it from Antwerp.[1]

Bede has a fame which is European as well as British. When Dante wrote of Paradise in *The Divine Comedy* 500 years later, Bede was the only Englishman in his procession of thinkers and philosophers.

His was an extraordinary accomplishment. He lived near Wallsend, the wall which marked the Roman boundary with the barbarian: for his contemporaries it seemed as though he was living near the world's end. He came from a people who had previously been illiterate pagans. He lived in a world without easy information retrieval – no reference libraries, computer networks or telephone. He did not even have a common language, for the Latin which was the medium of contemporary scholarship was not the ordinary language of the people.

Bede tried to be as careful as possible: he quizzed people who came his way, he examined documents whenever possible, he wrote asking questions. He operated as a modern historian would, sieving his sources, judging the worth of each, putting question marks when he was unsure. But he was much more than a chronicler. Bede was 'more learned in computation than any other scholar of his day'.[2] In particular he wrote *On the Computation of Time* in 725, about the time when he was writing the *History*, and he has the precision and care of someone interested in numbers: it was in part because of this that he was so concerned with the accurate dating of Easter and the liturgical year. Besides the *History* he wrote nearly 30 books, some biblical, some biographical, some hagiographical, which he carefully lists at the end of the *History*.

To this day the *Ecclesiastical History* reads well, convincing by its honesty and scholarship as well as by a certain endearing naivety. Bede is given to hero-worship and we approve of his choice of saints. He chronicles their doings and tells good stories.

He must have been a nice man. Many of the older commentators on his work fall under his spell: Stubbs, Bright and Plummer speak affectionately of him as a sort of saintly scholar-priest in the Victorian mould: he was conscientious, careful, interested in minutiae, a stay at home who wrote about great matters – almost an Oxbridge don. Such details as we know of his life have a homely quality. From the story of how, as a boy, only he and the abbot remained during the plague to sing the offices as a duet, to the account of his 'heavenly birthday' on 25 May 735, when he summoned his last strength to finish his translation of St John's Gospel, his life attracts us. But such beguiling detail must not blind us to his shortcomings.

He was not superhuman. We misread Bede if we fail to take into account his prejudices. He was strongly nationalistic, proud of the achievements of the English race and of the Northumbrians in particular. He was unwilling to hear well of others – especially the Welsh.

Further, he wrote with a purpose – to teach and to improve. During the time he was writing the *History* he sent a letter to the

Archbishop of York listing his complaints about the church of his day – it was too rich, there were too few bishops to cover the ground, too many priests and monks were ignorant, monasteries had become the property of laypeople. His ideal was simplicity. He delights in stories about Aidan preferring to walk rather than ride and in Cuthbert's heroic life of prayer. One of his models was Martin of Tours – ascetic, wholly committed to God, uncaring of himself. It is good to find that he followed this ideal himself: at his death he left behind only 'some pepper, some napkins and some incense'.

He consciously wrote for kings, showing that a ruler who lived well and followed the orthodox faith would succeed. He notes with approval that when Cenwalh of Sussex became a Christian he regained his kingdom, but when he expelled his bishop the kingdom was attacked. It is a simple lesson: God rewards his own and punishes those who disobey.

But his prime concern was the struggle for the unity and orthodoxy of the Church and the welfare of the people. In his history he shows that it is the hand of God which enables Roman order to calm pagan and Celtic chaos, brings peace to troubled peoples through godly kings and turns pagans into disciples of Christ. Those who brought war or who were heretical (i.e. not giving full allegiance to Rome) would suffer. Although a Christian, King Ecgfrith is scolded for making war on the Irish ('who had done him no harm') and his death at the hands of the Picts shortly afterwards is seen as just retribution. The monks of Bangor refused to accept the new Roman way of doing things, and there is an uncharacteristically peevish tone in Bede's description of their massacre by Aethelfrith a few years later. They had it coming to them.

For Bede, the Church had two levels. On the lower it was an all too human institution, involved in politics, holding meetings, making money. On the higher plane it was a company of saints whose spiritual prowess was shown by miracle and the powerful action of God, particularly over the evil spirits which inhabited such a hag-ridden corner of the pagan mind that their graves are filled with a protective jumble of amulets and charms.

 Michael Wallace-Hadrill points out that Bede was much more concerned with heresy than with paganism. We hear little of what pagans believed or practised, though he must have known much more about it than we do. However, he tells us much about those Christians who were resistant to Roman practices, for 'unity of discipline, as of doctrine, were for Bede a condition of survival of the Church'.[3] In a centrifugal age when all seemed to be fragmenting it looked as though uniformity was the way to survive.

It is this which makes him an authority to use with care in any account of the evangelisation of England. Rob Meens comments:

> As is well known Bede gives a biased account of the conversion of Anglo-Saxon England ... the Frankish contribution is not mentioned at all ... the continuity of the British church seems to have been stronger than Bede suggests and his statement that the Britons did nothing to convert the Angles and the Saxons should be regarded as an overstatement.[4]

Bede applauds all that comes from Rome via Canterbury and is dismissive of those who do not follow Roman ways. In part this is because he had much more access to Roman than to Celtic material (except the stories of the early Celtic missionaries in the north which he was well placed to record). In part it is because he is unsure of the reality of the Christianity which they offered – was a priest ordained by only one bishop a real priest offering real sacraments?

One example of this partiality is the conversion of Northumbria – something about which he must have known. He gives a strongly pro-Roman account centred upon Paulinus. A lesser writer, Nennius, gives an account of the success of Celtic missionaries in the area. Generally Bede is to be preferred to Nennius – he is a much more careful historian – but in this case such corroborative evidence as there is suggests that Nennius may have been right. At the very least Bede does not tell us the whole story: it is not that he lies, but rather that he plays down or omits what was favourable to the Celts and highlights the work of the Roman missionaries.

His attitude to the Celts and their beliefs was that their faith could be taken as true and even praiseworthy until the clear light of Rome was given to them. Ninian, Aidan, Columba and Cuthbert were the sort of saints he liked despite their Celtic pedigree – they lived simply, worked miracles, withstood kings, prayed much. However, after Whitby in 664, those Celts who did not conform to Roman ways became blameworthy for their obduracy and deserving of the punishment of God.

Bede longed for order. Not for nothing was he fascinated by numbers and computation. His history has a didactic aim – it is an account of the formation of a diocesan structure and the growth into unity of practice and doctrine of the English Church. His *History* ends with the Picts and the Irish being won round to Roman ways and organisation and only the perfidious Welsh hold out. For Bede the question was no longer open for it had become a matter of authority and to defy this was heresy and sin.

Because Bede is so outstanding as a historian there is a danger that his story is accepted as the whole truth. In fact it is only part of the truth. There is no Celtic Bede to put the other side. Bede wrote as a propagandist: most historians do. We must admire him and use him – but with care.

Notes

1 The Reformation was inevitably a time for hunting for historical roots. While the Catholics looked to Gregory and Rome, many Protestants traced their ancestry to Joseph of Arimathea who was reputed to have fled to England, bearing the Holy Grail, and preached the gospel to the inhabitants soon after the resurrection of Christ. He was supposed to have built the first English church at Glastonbury 43 years after the crucifixion, and William Blake saw him as 'one of the Gothic Artists who built the cathedrals in what we call the Dark Ages' (cf. Peter Ackroyd, *Blake*, 1995).

2 J. Campbell, *Essays in Anglo-Saxon History* (1986).

3 J. M. Wallace Hadrill, *Bede's Ecclesiastical History: A Commentary* (1988).

4 'A Background to Augustine's Mission to England', *Anglo-Saxon England* 23 (1994). On the other hand we should not be too hard on him. S. Basset in *Pastoral Care before the Parish* (1992) claims 'he notoriously disliked the British churches and wrote them out of his *Ecclesiastical History* as much as he could'; that may be true, but the real reason may simply have been that he did not have evidence of their doings far away in the South West where they were principally active. An examination of the places Bede refers to in his *History* shows that they are predominately in the East of the country: his sources in the West were much fewer.

Chapter 3

The Evangelisation of England

BY AD 600 England stuck out like a sore thumb. Since the (partial) conversion of the Goths and the other invading barbarians, it was the only part of the old Roman Empire which was pagan. It was surrounded on every side by Christian countries – Gaul, Scotland, Ireland, Wales.

It was from those four countries that the missionaries came – and from Rome. It is the latter which we know most about, because of the extraordinary contemporary documents in the Vatican, and the story as told by Bede. We will start with this but, as we have seen, it is far from being the whole story.

The Italian mission

It starts with Gregory. This extraordinary man had been a senior bureaucrat in Rome, then a monk, then a diplomat and administrator, finally Pope in 590. He was about 50 years old.

The position of Rome was precarious: the Lombards were threatening an invasion of Italy. The depopulated city was economically destitute and its past glories were only a shadow. The city had been the hub of the Christian faith to which all ecclesiastical power and scholarship and prayer had flowed. Now the old glories had almost entirely departed. The Eastern Church was drifting away from any acknowledgment of the centrality of Rome. The Patriarch of Constantinople had started to describe himself as 'universal bishop' in 588 and ecclesiastical power had begun to drain away to the East along with the political power that Rome once had wielded.

As Pope, Gregory was not only a religious leader but also the secular ruler of the city. There had been no Emperor in Rome for more than a century, and because of the vacuum of authority the Pope had assumed the role of administrator of the city. Among the amazing 850 letters from Gregory which still exist there are many which organise wheat shipments from Sicily, deal with the cleanliness of the streets and berate local government officials for idleness.

Idleness was not one of Gregory's vices. Nor was lack of vision. A letter of 599 shows that the mission to the English had been long in his mind, for they were 'placed in the corner of the world and until this time worshipping sticks and stones'. He had 'given long thought to it', probably because he had been asked to consider going there himself by Benedict I (574–578). It was even rumoured that he had set out to evangelise England – but a locust had settled on him and the words *Sta in loco* ('stay where you are') had come to him: clearly Bede thought it was an unlikely story, but it is certain that in 595 Gregory wrote to a priest in Gaul asking him to buy some young Anglo-Saxon slaves so that they could be put in a monastery and be trained as missionaries to their own country.

The mission to England was part of a wider dream. Gregory's aim covered the whole of the world as it was then known. Liam de Peor says that he looked for 'the restoration of the western Roman Empire: but in his vision the new legions would be priests and monks'.[1] To do this he had to show that Rome was interested in even the farthest flung places, especially when they were pockets of paganism.

We know that he was also anxious about the Irish. In a world where everything was falling apart it was important that there should be unity and continuity. As a true Roman, Gregory tried to enforce uniformity in liturgy, ecclesiastical behaviour and doctrine. The Eastern Church was bad enough with its differing practices and what he regarded as semi-heretical teaching: Gregory was a fervent disciple of Augustine of Hippo and the Eastern Church had not adopted his theology. The Irish were even more difficult, though their numbers were smaller. They also had failed to benefit from Augustine, their keeping of ecclesiastical rules was lax to say the least and they were notoriously ill-disciplined. Even

worse, they clearly had an appeal to others. Columbanus had come
from Ireland to Gaul in about 590 and was busy founding Celtic
monasteries in Gaul and even in Italy and beyond. In each monastery Celtic practices were normal and soon he was to have a
quarrel with Gregory over the date on which Easter was to be
kept. Columbanus was only the best known – all over Europe
Irish monks were founding communities. Gregory must have
regarded the Celts as the wild men from the west – coming from
outside the boundaries of the old Empire and causing confusion.

But it would unfair to claim that Gregory's mission to England
was merely a political move. As a man who had sold his ancestral
home and founded seven monasteries with the proceeds, he had a
genuine love of the gospel and a longing to see it spread to the
ends of the earth. The story about Gregory seeing Angle slaves in
the market and calling them angels is highly dubious, but it
shows the character of the man – caring, vigorous, visionary. He
also thought that he was pushing at an open door – while organis-
ing Augustine's mission he wrote in a letter, 'It has come to our
ears that by the mercy of God the English race earnestly desire to
be converted to the Christian faith . . .'.[2]

Gregory chose Augustine as his rather unlikely Billy Graham.
He knew him well, for Augustine had been the administrator
and disciplinarian of Gregory's own monastery. He gave him full
backing by sending 40 people with him – in contrast with many
modern evangelistic ventures, Augustine had good resources.[3]

Gregory gave him instructions. He was to found twelve dioceses, with archbishoprics at London and York following the pattern of government left by the Roman legions nearly two centuries
earlier. Augustine and his band set out in 596. They were held up
in Gaul and wrote to Gregory confessing they were 'afraid . . . for
they were appalled at the idea of going to a barbarous, fierce and
pagan nation'.[4] They wanted to come back. Gregory did not
approve of such pusillanimity and, in the circumstances, wrote a
surprisingly patient and understanding letter to them. However
the nub of it is an order to 'carry out this holy task'.

The party eventually landed in Thanet in midsummer 597.[5] They
met Ethelbert, the king of Kent, and received a remarkably good
welcome. Not for the last time a king's wife had prepared the
ground. Bertha was a Christian and even had a bishop with her

as chaplain. Ethelbert allowed Augustine the use of the ruined
church of St Martin's in Canterbury. It had already been used by
Bertha and was a relic of the Christian church of the fourth and
fifth century – a vivid reminder of the fact that Christians had
been around before.

It all seemed to be remarkably easy, and their early fears ground-
less. A trickle of converts came in and then a flood – including
Ethelbert himself.[6] How large was the flood? Gregory, writing to
the Patriarch of Alexandria in 598, says triumphantly that 'more
than 10,000 Englishmen are reported to be baptized' at Christmas
597. If so, it was remarkable growth for a mission begun so
nervously six months before. However modern claims for evangelistic events suggest that we should be cautious about large round
numbers. Bede is suspiciously silent on the subject. Clearly the
mission was going well, but we need to beware of excessive claims,
especially when these are coupled with a request for more
resources: evangelists know well that church leaders prefer to
encourage success rather than prop up failure.

In 601 two monks returned to Rome saying that things were
going so well that more evangelists were needed. The warm welcome given in Kent had had repercussions because Ethelbert was
the most powerful ruler south of the Humber, and it seemed as if
those kings who were subject to him would also welcome missionaries. Gregory agreed that help should be given, and a second party
was sent. The significance of this reinforcement of the mission to
England can be gauged by the fact that only five people were sent
from Rome in the succeeding four and a half centuries.[7]

The early successes were followed through by the conversion
of King Sigebert of the East Saxons in 604, who in gratitude built
the first St Paul's in his capital of London. Another diocese was
founded at Rochester and all seemed well. Then a pattern which
was to become all too familiar happened. Ethelbert died in 616
and the accession of his pagan son meant that paganism swept
back. Many relapsed. The bishopric of London had to be abandoned and its bishop and the Bishop of Rochester fled to Gaul.
Archbishop Lawrence was about to follow and legend has it that
he was prevented by a vision (more probably, by a change in the
political situation). If he had gone it is likely that the Roman

mission would have collapsed. The Christian faith hung on but only just and in a very limited area.

Nine years later it sprang up far away in a new form. Once again a king's wife was the starting point. Ethelbert's daughter was a Christian and she was to be married to Edwin, the King of Northumbria and the most powerful ruler in England. In the negotiations before her marriage it had been agreed that she should be allowed to practise her faith and bring her own priests with her. As a result Paulinus was consecrated bishop and accompanied her north for her wedding in 625. A year's preaching brought little fruit but in early 626 Edwin narrowly escaped assassination by a poisoned dagger, and shortly afterward his baby daughter was born safely. He began the journey of faith. At Pentecost 626 he allowed his baby and eleven other people in the court to be baptised. Further, he said that he would become a Christian himself if he won a battle against the West Saxons who had tried to assassinate him. He beat them comprehensively but still hesitated, realising that the conversion of a king had political consequences. He held a meeting with his counsellors at which there was much argument including the vivid account given by one of the chieftains of the pagan view of human life – a sparrow flying briefly into the warmth of an Anglo-Saxon hall and then as quickly disappearing, 'but of what is to follow or what went before we are entirely ignorant'. The debate was dramatically ended when the pagan high priest Coifi renounced his faith and profaned his own temple. Edwin was baptised on Easter Day 627 at Goodmanham, a little to the east of York.

Paulinus then began a widespread evangelistic campaign which lasted for six years. Bede describes him as a 'a man tall of stature, a little stooping, with black hair and a thin face, a hooked and thin nose, his aspect both venerable and awe-inspiring'. He travelled throughout the kingdom of Northumbria – at that time stretching from the Humber to southern Scotland, and crossed the border into Lincolnshire, converting the leader of the city of Lincoln.

But once again it did not last. In 633 Edwin was killed by Penda of Mercia and Northumbria reverted to paganism.[8] Paulinus, with Edwin's widow, fled to Kent. It seemed as though once again the Christian faith had only its toehold in the South East. Paulinus had started to build a church in York – years later Wilfred found it decayed and unused, with its roof leaking, no glass in the windows and the walls smeared by nesting birds. It was a symbol of an enterprise which had started with such high hopes but appeared to have been crushed. Obviously feeling that the recovery of his bishopric in York was impossible, Paulinus became Bishop of Rochester and died there ten years later. His successor at Rochester was Ithamar – the first Anglo-Saxon bishop. Previously all bishops had been Italian. It was ceasing to be an Italian mission and becoming an indigenous church. The pattern repeated by many younger churches today had taken place – the leadership of the foreign missionaries was giving way to that of the native-born. However, it was to be many years before an English archbishop was appointed.

By the 630s it appeared that great initial evangelistic success had been short-lived. Forty years after Augustine landed there seemed to be little to show for it. There was a foothold in Kent but little else, for even the diocese of London had been reclaimed for paganism. 'The Italian mission to Kent appears to have been relatively unsuccessful after its first few years and the leading role from the 630s seems to have been taken by the Irish mission which came to Lindisfarne from Iona.'[9]

The Celtic mission

In relating the story of the mission from Rome we are on firm ground. The sources are reasonably plentiful and reasonably reliable. Details are disputed but the overall pattern is clearly seen.

Looking at the Celtic mission to the English is like peering through a mist. The best recorded glimpse, because of Bede, is the mission in Northumbria. But it is likely that the other movements which came from Ireland, Wales and Gaul were at least as important.

One thing is obvious. There was no such thing as 'the Celtic church'. Too many writers speak of 'Celtic' practices, theology and doings as though the churches which existed among the Celts were as uniform and well organised as the church in Rome. We should think of them as enormously varied. Some Celtic Christian communities were comparatively structured and cohesive while others were the result of individual private enterprise. As Ian Bradley says:

> To speak of a Celtic Church suggests a degree of organisation and institutionalisation which was not there. Celtic Christianity was much more of a loose federation of virtually autonomous confederations. Maybe it was not even that but rather a shifting pattern of essentially provisional attitudes, images and structures which wove their way round one another and around the culture and society of which they were so much a part in the manner of the interlacing ribbons in the Celtic knot...[10]

Candida Casa

The first significant place we know of in the Celtic world is Whithorn in South East Scotland. By tradition it was in 398, that is, 200 years before Augustine came to Canterbury, that Nynia (Ninian) founded the monastery there which became known as Candida Casa. The limewashed walls which gave the place its nickname have recently been excavated.[11] Certainly there was a very early Christian settlement there and its influence was felt throughout the region, as can be seen by the number of gravestones with a similar Christian design in southern Scotland. Significantly the monastery was dedicated to St Martin of Tours. Since Martin was barely dead in 398 it is most likely a later ascription, but this dedication still indicates the type of monasticism Candida Casa had come to represent, and deliberately linked this far-off outpost of Christianity with the main monastic movement (cf. Chapter 5). Certainly Candida Casa was likely to have been one of the main routes by which the great monastic tradition crossed the few miles of sea which separate Galloway from Ireland.

Ireland

Ireland had never been conquered by the Romans: it was outside the Empire. Nevertheless it received the Christian gospel and was part of the Christianity centred upon Rome – it spoke in Latin, it followed the practices of the Fathers, it looked to the Pope as the leader of the Church. As early as 429 the Pope sent Palladius as a bishop to 'those of the Irish who believe in Christ'. So there were Christians in Ireland before Patrick came, though it was he who came to be seen as the great missionary: even today we read that

Patrick 'single-handedly converted the people of Ireland'.[12] This is untrue, for central and southern Ireland had long had Christian missionaries – only in the north where Patrick went had there been little penetration. Patrick was born into a Christian family about 390 possibly in Birdoswald on Hadrian's Wall, was captured by pirates and taken to Ireland as a slave. After six years he escaped and wandered as far as Gaul and possibly Rome. After consecration as a bishop he returned to Ireland as a missionary, dying in 461.[13] At this stage the Irish church had a Roman form and there was as much communication between Ireland and Rome as the troubled state of Europe allowed. However as political conditions deteriorated still further towards the end of the fifth century Ireland became virtually cut off, a backwater which pursued its own way without reference to Rome or anywhere else.

During this shadowy time there occurred a massive and most significant change. Patrick had continued to establish the normal Roman diocesan pattern, but only a few years after his death the Irish church changed its organisation. Monasteries displaced dioceses as the basic unit and abbots became more powerful than bishops. The monastery became not only a centre for prayer and learning but the heart of the organisation of the church and extraordinarily evangelistic. The story of Celtic evangelism is not about the extension of a diocesan structure but about the expansion of communities. The Celts did not church-plant; they monastery-planted.

Columba

The best known, because best documented, mission was from Ireland to England via Scotland. Columba (Columcille = dove) had a far from dove-like past before he set off for Scotland. A chieftain's son, he was an early victim of the laws governing copyright. The traditional story is that he borrowed without permission a valuable copy of St Finnian's version of the psalms (possibly the newly translated Vulgate) and copied it by night secretly. He was brought to trial before the High King Diarmeid and condemned with the lapidary sentence: 'To every cow its calf, and to every book its copy'. Columba was so incensed that he raised his clan and, wielding the copied psalms as a banner, fought a battle against the High King which he won and at which 3,000 people were killed. It is a good story and parts may be true – there certainly was a battle of Culdrevny in which he was involved – but clearly Ireland was becoming too hot for him, and this warrior-priest may have thought it wise to go on pilgrimage – the 'white martyrdom' of the Celts by which they sought some lonely place for meditation and prayer.

Columba and his twelve companions landed in Iona in 563. It was already a pagan holy place and many of the standing stones there are pre-Christian megaliths which have been baptised into Christ by having a fish or chi-rho symbol carved on them. Columba built a monastery on the site of the pagan temple. It is an unlikely headquarters for a major missionary movement for it was on the edge of the Kingdom of Dalriada which was largely composed of Irish people who had settled in western and southern Scotland. It was primarily to these people that the Iona missionaries went, though it is known that they also went further east to the Picts. Initially missionaries went to the royal households; sometimes the king and court were converted, but even if this did not happen the king might be prepared at least to tolerate evangelistic preaching in his realm. Quickly the area, much of which had already been touched by work from Whithorn, became largely Christian.

Columba died on 9 June 597 – possibly within days, certainly within months, of Augustine landing at Thanet. By that time there was a solid Christian base in western Scotland.

So far the Iona mission had been to the Celts. At this point Anglo-Saxon England became involved. When the reigning king of Northumbria was defeated in 616 by Edwin his family fled north, some taking refuge in Iona. There Prince Oswald was baptised. As we have seen, following the death of Edwin in 633 there was reversion to paganism, and Paulinus and the queen left hurriedly. However, after a year of chaos Oswald gained the throne, winning the battle of Heavenfield. His faith meant much to him – before the battle he set up a wooden cross and after the victory he at once asked for missionaries to be sent to his kingdom. It was a momentous choice. In not turning to the Roman missionaries, as might have been expected after the exertions of Paulinus in Northumbria, Oswald changed the direction of missionary work in England. He went back to the Celts among whom he had grown up, and asked Iona to send a missionary to establish the Christian faith. The first evangelist who was sent did not suit so he was returned as a reject, grumbling as he went that 'they were an uncivilised people of an obstinate and barbarous temperament'.[14] In his place Iona sent Aidan. He founded a monastery at Lindisfarne – near the royal palace at Bamburgh, but not too close. Like its mother-house it became a centre of missionary work.

From Lindisfarne not only Northumbria but many other parts of England were evangelised. We know something of those who worked closely with the royal households. Chad worked in Mercia – invited there in 653 by the pagan Penda who had mellowed with age – and established his see at Lichfield. Cedd, his brother, travelled down to Essex and worked among the East Saxons. These names reverberate. But there were many others, who founded Christian communities in place after place and whose names we do not know. In the middle of the seventh century there was a great advance of Christian belief. The position had looked desperate after Paulinus was chased from Northumbria. In the event the Celtic mission took over where the Roman mission had petered out and was successful and, above all, enduring. There were no more widespread relapses into paganism.

Evangelism from the East
Before the mission from Lindisfarne there was an earlier and extraordinary mission from Ireland to England of which we know only a little. This time it came via Gaul. Columbanus was a monk in the monastery in Bangor in Northern Ireland. Around 590 he was allowed to go on pilgrimage with twelve other monks. They went far into the semi-evangelised area of northern France and founded a monastery at Annegray near Strasburg – once again following the common Celtic practice of rebuilding a pagan temple. Despite the austere vegetarian regime it grew fast and soon spawned other monasteries in the area. However in 610 Columbanus, like John the Baptist and St John Chrysostom, criticised the morals of the royal family. It is never a safe thing to do, and the Irish were ordered to return to Ireland. In the event they dispersed to northern France and Switzerland, establishing communities wherever they went, including the famous monastery

of St Gall. Columbanus himself pressed on into northern Italy and founded Bobbio in 614.[15]

Columbanus was the most famous, but there were other Irish monks flooding across the continent. At this time we know of Irish monasteries being founded in Vienna and even as far east as Poland and Romania and as far south as Taranto. Naturally they followed their normal Celtic liturgical customs and teaching, and it is not surprising that Gregory I was alarmed at the spread of their practices.[16]

One centre of Columbanian missionary work was Burgundy. It is probable that it was from there that East Anglia was evangelised, as well as by Fursey and his brothers who also came directly from Ireland about 633. Once again there was a knock-on effect. The monasteries set up by Fursey and his companions founded daughter communities near Chichester and at Malmesbury and other places in southern England. Once again we can see how limited was the area evangelised from Kent, though Celtic and Roman missionaries worked together in some areas, apparently amicably.

One indirect form of evangelism from Columbanus was the education of royal personages. Clearly the monastic schools in Gaul had a reputation and Saxon kings often sent their children, especially their daughters, for education. Often they returned as Christians and influenced their families, and continued the impressive contribution made by queens to the evangelization of England.

Other missionary activities are barely visible in the mists. There is the likelihood that the Welsh Christians – a mixture of native Welsh and those British who had been squeezed westward by the Anglo-Saxon invasions – evangelised much of the West Country, and the ubiquitous Irish monks seem to have been everywhere – a Celtic cross there, a church named after a Celtic saint there, an echo of Irish practice somewhere else.

Conclusion

All in all it has to be said that the Celts were the main evangelists of England. The monastic pattern seems to have been more successful at evangelising the society in which they were set. The Roman pattern of parishes and dioceses, as we shall see later, may well be the most suitable for settled communities and a commonly accepted faith. The question which seventh-century evangelists faced, and which the Church today faces, is whether it is an appropriate organisation for a non-Christian or semi-Christian situation. The comparative failure of the mission of Augustine may be due to the Roman desire to set up an organisation before Augustine and his companions had gathered a people of faith. The letters of the Popes and the writings of Bede show the extreme importance they gave to structure. Even allowing for the concern which ecclesiastical authority always has for things to be done properly, the emphasis on the bishop and his authority seems excessive.

The Roman pattern was to set up a skeleton organisation and then evangelise. The Celtic pattern was to gather the people and then set up an appropriate framework for them.

Whatever the reason the Celtic Church became highly evangelistic. They set out to spread the gospel, and in the second half of the sixth century, well before Augustine landed they were venturing for Christ. It was not a co-ordinated campaign. Individuals and communities set out to spread the faith because they were excited by the gospel.

Notes

1 *The Making of Britain: The Dark Ages* (1984).
2 Presumably he had heard of the openness of the English to the gospel from Bishop Liudhard who had been acting as chaplain to Queen Bertha, the wife of Ethelbert of Kent.
3 A discussion of Gregory's policy can be found in an article by R. A. Markus in *The Mission of the Church and the Propagation of the Faith* (1970).
4 *Ecclesiastical History* 1.23.
5 Like everything else in Anglo-Saxon history there are contrary views: some think he landed in late 596: cf. P. H. Blair, *The World of Bede* (2nd edn 1990).
6 The date of Ethelbert's conversion is uncertain: all we can say is that it was before his death in 616, though a letter written to him by Gregory I in 601 strongly suggests that he was already a Christian by then.
7 One of these was Birinus who was sent by Pope Honorius I on a roving commission to preach the gospel to the heathen. Landing in Sussex he found enough heathen to satisfy him and settled there, leading the king to faith in 635 and establishing his see at Dorchester. Interestingly this

one-man mission seems to have been instigated without reference to Paulinus and the other bishops in England at the time. Perhaps it was seen as a new venture – the middle of the 630s were a time of defeat and retreat for the Christian cause and the Pope may have thought that a new independent attempt had to be made. It is a curious footnote to the mission from Rome.

8   Penda made a habit of killing kings who had become Christians: besides Edwin he killed Osfrid and Eadfrid, Awald, Sigebehrt, Egric and Anna.

9   James Campbell, *Essays in Anglo-Saxon History* (1986).

10   *The Celtic Way* (1993).

11   See the Excavation Reports. For a radical reassessment of the Whithorn evidence, which suggests that there was no early monastery, see Charles Thomas, *Whithorn's Christian Beginnings* (1992).

12   Robert Van de Weyer, *Celtic Fire.*

13   Needless to say the details of Patrick's life are disputed. The link with Birdoswald is uncertain: some put his dates as *c.* 415–490. His autobiographical *Confession* is a fine account of the life of a humble and Christ-centred person but it is tantalizingly short of facts! As Professor Geároid MacNiocaill delightfully expresses it in *Ireland before the Vikings* it 'affords splendid opportunities for conjecture and abundant scope for the exercise of academic spleen'.

14   *Ecclesiastical History* 3.5 – not the last time an evangelist has blamed failure on the people he was sent to.

15   It may not be too fanciful to ascribe St Francis' love of natural things in parts to the Celtic overtones of the monastery which meant so much to him. There are several legends of Columbanus which tell of his rapport with creatures, including one in which twelve wolves stood in an patient circle while he finished a psalm, and then went their way.

16   A useful map showing the Irish foundations can be found in Ray Simpson's *Exploring Celtic Spirituality* (1995). It shows 45 monasteries, and there were more.

Chapter 4

The New Evangelism

THE EARLY missionaries found a country whose spiritual roots were uncertain. Their old gods were the gods of fire and earth and water, of thunder and lightening. They seemed appropriate in their homelands of Northern Europe, but did they work across the sea? Would the tricks of Loki or the reverberations of Thor still have an effect in this new country?

Western Europe today is also unsure of its intellectual and spiritual roots. The old certainties of the Enlightenment are fading fast. Science is no longer seen as a bringer of benefits which will lead to a new age of rationality and hope, but as a will-o-the-wisp which has led us astray into a mechanised wilderness in which human beings feel alien intruders. The old 'certainties' of modernism derived from the Enlightenment are being assailed by the diverse battalions of post-modernism. The 'clockwork universe' in which everything, including human behaviour, happened in a direct line of cause and effect has been shown to be mistaken. Chaos theory shows how massive, unpredictable happenings can result from minute disturbances. The 'Uncertainty Principle' shows that at the atomic level not all things can be forecasted. The coolly predictable universe of the world-view which began more than a century ago is being replaced. Astronomy shows us a universe full of movement and change, and new wonders of black holes, pulsars and the like. Nor is this restricted to the physical world. Post-modernism takes the humanity of people seriously and delights in fun and an attitude of wonder and exploration: the child in each of us is not to be eclipsed by the adult but is to be incorporated into a complete human being. Like the Bible it sees the human being as holistic and is suspicious of any artificial categorisation. It is from this that the enormous interest in 'alternative medicine' and the ecological thinking about the oneness of creation stems. In New Age thinking this is carried further into a semi-religion.

The rapidity of technological progress makes our heads reel with questions. Do the ethical dilemmas produced by medical advances or biological engineering come so fast that we cannot come to a mind on what is right and wrong? Does modern farming give us what we want or merely create a productive prairie and cruelty to animals on a vast and hidden scale? Do the computer and the information revolution open up a world of work which gives much to some and unemployment to others? Our legal system, our theology, our political and economic life and our understanding of ourselves as human beings puff far behind the juggernaut which we have set in motion and seem powerless to stop or steer.

Post-modernism seems to be a way out. Whereas modernism was strictly rational, the new ways of thinking are fuzzy, suspicious of logical thinking, unsure of 'progress'. Modernism seems to be cold and cerebral; post-modernism seems to claim back humanity by injecting a sense of choice and even playfulness.

Terry Eagleton, one of the intellectual gurus of the new thinking says,

> We are now in the process of waking from the nightmare of modernity, with its manipulative reason and fetish of totality, into the laid-back pluralism of the post-modern, that heterogeneous range of life styles and language games which has renounced the nostalgic urge to totalise and legitimate itself.

Another writer, Neil Smith, says in oft-quoted words, 'The enlightenment is dead, Marxism is dead, the working class movement is dead . . . and the author does not feel very well either!'

Is this a real escape or simply a way of avoiding the harshness of the questions? Is it a psychological withdrawal into unreality because of the pressures of modern society? It is clearly more securely based than the 'flower power' of the sixties but is it the start of a whole new way of looking at the world or simply a passing intellectual fashion? This remains to be seen, but the rise of a post-modern atmosphere increasingly pervades all of society and dictates the way we think. Whether the new way of thinking produces acceptable answers is uncertain: what is clear is that its criticism of modernism is well-founded.

The challenge of post-modernism

The new ways of thinking which come under the umbrella of post-modernism have consequences for the Christian evangel.

First, post-modernism has a deep distrust of 'meta-narratives'.[1] By this is meant any overarching belief-system which purports to explain the cosmos. Thus modernism spoke of 'the scientific world-view' – a way of looking at the world which embraced all of human existence. Such a concept is rejected by post-modernism which emphasises differences rather than similarities. It wants to rejoice in the diversity of thought rather than see all things brought into one schema. Hence the rejection of Marxism and doctrinaire approaches to politics from either Right or Left, for they also are meta-narratives.

The same rejection of the wide-angled lens of a meta-narrative applies to religion. Most world religions have their own all-embracing (and widely differing) viewpoints. Whether it is a belief in the Nordic gods or a belief in Christianity or Islam is immaterial – they are all to be discarded for there is no such thing as an explanation of all things.

Thus while the Christian faith may rejoice in the abolition of the cold precisions of modernism and the values of the Enlightenment against which it has struggled for so long, the new way of thinking also has its challenges. The Christian faith may rejoice in the new acceptance of humanity and diversity but it has to realise that it is sidelined into being merely another in the long queue of 'viewpoints' which are all equally valued and all equally distrusted.

The same suspicion of meta-narratives applies to ethical systems. Such compendium words like 'justice' or 'honesty' are thought to be impositions which avoid argument – how a person behaves is to be worked out personally and not imposed by social conformity or a religious framework like the Ten Commandments.

It is because of this that religious pluralism in society has been welcomed and the New Age movement has sprung up. Post-modernism says 'Let a thousand flowers bloom' – and you may pick a bunch of flowers which come from many different sources. You may accept an ethical stance from one faith, a belief in life after death from another and a guru from a collection of notables which can include Jesus and Buddha and Mr Moon. These leaders have no universal significance but are merely speakers on behalf of a particular interest group and to be awarded no higher status.

Post-modernism also has an attitude to history and tradition which is non-biblical. The past is to be discarded and the explanations of historians are untrustworthy, not least because they so often exclude whole areas of human existence – women, the poor, the non-European. The Christian faith, like most world religions, is rooted in the past, depends upon historical narratives and upon a certain explanation of them.

Post-modernism has been criticised as a philosophy of the consumer society. As Graham Cray has said: 'Tesco ergo sum' – 'I shop therefore I am'. It elevates the autonomous individual in his or her search for meaning, encourages every viewpoint but turns shuddering from any idea of truth, is both attracted by commitment but shies away from it. It is the philosophy of most of the media: all things are interesting provided they can be packaged into a programme.

It is against this backdrop of a rapidly changing world-view that the churches decided that the 1990s should be a Decade of Evangelism.[2]

The Decade of Evangelism

The Decade began in January 1991. By 1996 we can see that it has been a success – in one sense. Far more people in the churches are thinking evangelistically; some are even putting their thoughts into practice. The Church of England has probably been more affected than most, and in every diocese there is an emphasis on reaching out to communities and individuals. The Turnbull Commission on the reform of the central structures of the Church of England puts mission as its central motive for change – though acknowledging that financial pressures have given urgency to their enquiries. Mission sets the agenda; finance dictates the timescale.[3] There has been a marked change of attitude within the churches.

In another sense the Decade has been less successful. Attendance at church on Sunday has not begun to rise significantly. Numbers have declined in most of the denominations since the beginning of the century, but there are grounds for moderate numerical hope. The rate of decline in regular church attenders has slowed down and stopped during the past ten years in the non-Roman Catholic churches. Some are showing signs of growth. However the Roman Catholic Church, which had maintained its attendances well until the early 1980s, appears to have begun a period of considerable decline in mass attendance.[4] But we must beware of allowing the media's wish for us to produce 'bums on pews' to dictate our own evaluation of the Decade. The Church is not a business corporation and cannot be judged in commercial terms. We should avoid the slick PR which points to success stories and hides the areas where there is no growth. Tempting though it is for us to blow our own trumpet, knowing well that no one will blow it for us, it is a temptation to be resisted – floating down from the Temple rock assures one of today's headlines but does not build for eternity.

If we attempt to increase regular attendance we are trying to do something very difficult – buck a sociological trend. In all social groupings those organisations which rely upon regular participation have experienced a drop in numbers. Thus the British Legion, the Women's Institute and active trades unionism have all declined sharply. Student unions in universities find it difficult to attract members, let alone subscriptions. Conversely bodies which mean commitment to a cause without regular attendance have shown very considerable growth – the National Trust and the Royal Society for the Protection of Birds have expanded explosively.

The 'New Evangelism'

In the 1990s few have wished to copy old patterns of evangelism. At the beginning of the Decade a few wanted Billy Graham to be invited back, but there was little enthusiasm. The possibility of a visit from Luis Palau was turned down by church leaders as inappropriate. Stadium evangelism of that kind has not been seen as the right way forward. The church leaders were right, for it has to be said that when this type of evangelism has been tried in recent years it has failed. In 1994 four major initiatives were taken by various bodies. On the admission of the organisers the JIM ('Jesus in me') initiative produced few tangible results. The ecumenical Lent course 'Have Another Look' attracted few of the hoped-for non-churchgoers. 'Minus to Plus' distributed evangelistic material free: the number of returns which led on to faith was tiny despite the £5 million expenditure. Only the Pentecost celebration, 'On Fire', could be said to be even partially successful, and that was disrupted by the weather. Signs of Life, an evaluation produced by the Church of England, concludes: 'The overall impression of these four events is that they were limited in their effectiveness. Enormous amounts of effort by many church members and vast sums of money were expended with limited impact.'[5]

Ten years ago such methods of evangelism would probably have had a limited success, as did the Billy Graham meetings of the mid-1980s. It appears that in a remarkably short time – the first five years of the Decade – the pattern of evangelism in England has changed. How?

It is a remarkable fact that the 'New Evangelism' seems to have evolved spontaneously in many different denominations and without any central planning. It is a sea-change which has altered both the practice and the attitudes of the churches in the space of barely five years. Many of older forms of evangelism are suddenly felt to be largely inappropriate and ineffective and new patterns are taking their place. It is interesting that it has happened in the first five years of the Decade, but it may be no more than coincidental – or it may be God's way of making his Church more effective in the new situation which faces it.

At present we are in the middle of the change and it is difficult to evaluate. In the perspective of history it may turn out to be the reaction of the churches to the era of the 1990s as they realise the more overtly post-Christian stance of those they are ministering to, the rise of post-modernist thinking and a more realistic view of the place of the Church in modern society.

There are three main areas of change. None of them are wholly new but the alteration in emphasis is remarkable. In each case it is a move from a 'Roman' to a more 'Celtic' way of doing things:

1. from the Damascus road to the road to Emmaus;
2. from doctrine to spirituality;
3. from mission to missions.

1. From the Damascus road to the road to Emmaus

The controlling biblical paradigm of conversion has been the story of the conversion of St Paul on his way to Damascus. The story occurs three times in the book of Acts and has been turned to often as an example of what conversion to the Christian faith should be like – a sudden, overwhelming, experience of God.

Historically evangelicals believed in a 'moment of conversion'. They used methods of evangelism which expected that there would be a specific time when a person became a Christian. Hence the urgent wish to 'lead someone to Christ' – whether this was in a large crowd exhorted by an evangelist 'while every head is bowed' or in one-to-one witness. It assumed that people had little previous spiritual life and that they were not Christian before this moment. The 'new evangelism', while accepting that sudden conversions occur, also makes space for those who come to Christ over a period of time. The shift to a more gradual model of coming to faith has taken place for several reasons. First and foremost, Christians have begun to evaluate and learn from past experience. British research in the early 1990s suggested that church-centred, event-orientated methods were largely ineffective. The comments above about the four events in 1994 showed that this was correct: these methods may have worked in the past but they have limited effect today – hence the frequent comment after a mission: 'It did not bring many people in, but it did us a power of good'. Much of this style of evangelism has a North American base but there is a different sociological and religious background there. In the USA a considerable proportion of the population has a residuary knowledge of the Christian faith and people can respond emotionally and intellectually to what the evangelist is talking about. When someone has an intellectual knowledge of the Christian faith what is often required is that they should make an act of will to 'follow Christ' – not an intellectual assent but an act of volitional acceptance. The pressure of being part of large group, the emotional content to the 'message' and the 'appeal' help people to take the step of saying 'I will'. Such people are not put off by ecclesiastical surroundings (and massed choirs in a big stadium can be as 'religious' as cathedral evensong). The people who went forward at Billy Graham rallies were nearly all people who had some previous connection with a church. Mass evangelism works with the half-converted – though the mild manipulation which can be part of it has to be accepted.

Second, detailed research has now been done in England on the way in which individual adults come to faith. This has shown that 69 per cent come gradually to faith rather than through a sudden conversion. Further, a close study of the people who have a 'sudden conversion' shows that it is often an episode in a gradual process rather than a sudden turning to God. However, most evangelistic methods assume that someone who responds will do so suddenly and leap into a sudden confession of Christ as Lord and Saviour.

This research should not be misread. It does *not* say that all people have a gradual conversion. Overall, 31 per cent of the people interviewed said that they could name the day on which they 'found Christ' – and these were by no means limited to evangelical churches: one in five of those from 'non-evangelical' churches had had such a sudden conversion.

So while it is true that a sizable minority of people have a 'Pauline' conversion the majority do not. For them the biblical paradigm is not the Damascus road but the story of the two disciples on the road to Emmaus.

This narrative in Luke 24 portrays a gradual opening up of faith. The two downcast men are walking away from Jerusalem – they are leaving the centre of faith. A stranger draws near and starts to talk, accompanying them on their journey. The stranger begins to speak of the person of Jesus and teaches them the tradition from the Scriptures. Realisation comes as the stranger breaks the bread in the familiar sacramental action. The Stranger, now recognised as God in action, then disappears. The couple turn and hurry back to the church gathered in Jerusalem.

This portrayal of the spiritual journey is the story of so many modern people. They walk slowly away from the Church and then find that a Stranger draws near to them. His identity is not revealed but he goes along with them through their life. Slowly things begin to make sense until they begin to recognise that God has been with them all the time. They have been within the orbit of Word and Sacrament all the time although they were not aware of it. The Stranger who is the revealer then leaves them elated, puzzled and eager for more as they re-enter the community of faith.

2.   From doctrine to spirituality

Post-modernist thinking is uneasy about claims that anything is absolute truth. On the other hand human experience is seen as having validity whether or not it can be verified in any way.

The same tendency to elevate experience above dogma is seen in people's approach to God.

Traditionally spiritual life flowed out of and was a consequence of doctrine. You believed certain things about God and as a result prayed and lived in a certain way. Today that is often reversed. People may have an experience which they interpret as having a spiritual content – and the Alister Hardy Institute say that 63 per cent of people have had at least one such episode in their lives.[6] It is from those episodes that they construct a theology. Because of little or inadequate teaching they have few reference points and the constructs can be weird indeed. INFORM, the group which looks at 'New Religious Movements', says that there are 1,600 NRMs in the British Isles. One person I met had encountered some literature from the Aetherius Society. It contained a prediction which seemed to him to come true; as a result he joined the Society which claims that if you send money to someone in Surrey you will receive a newsheet telling of what will come to pass on planet Earth. This information comes from someone on Venus. Since that planet has an atmosphere of boiling sulphuric acid this seems to be intrinsically unlikely. But because his first encounter with the Aetherius Society was positive, this English graduate decided that the rest of the teaching must be true. The same process is true of those who believe in astrology or crystallomancy or the multitudinous forms of alternative medicine. If you try homeopathy and you think that it is helpful to you, you will be disposed to accept the philosophy that lies behind it. Experience leads to doctrine – not the other way round.

We may deplore this and say that truth should be a necessary control and referee of experience, but the present reality is otherwise. We may claim that people are prying into mistaken and even spiritually dangerous places but we will not be listened to. Spiritual experience is seen as the touchstone of truth – not the reverse. The same process can be seen within the Christian Church. People with little Christian teaching who encounter the Christian Church positively in one of its traditions tend to accept the doctrinal and cultural presuppositions of that grouping – whether it is Catholic or Protestant or Charismatic – and only slowly realise that there is a much wider field of faith.

Christians should be more prepared to explain the spiritual life they have already begun to enjoy than to seek to persuade others of doctrinal truth. Like Paul on Mars Hill in Athens the task is to introduce them to the 'the Unknown God' whom they have already encountered, rather than to persuade them of the truth of the faith. The doctrinal undergirding has to come, but only after God has been encountered. For many years non-western Christians have been telling us that the Church in Europe and America is too cerebral and insufficiently attuned to the emotions and human experience; now the people amongst whom we live are telling us the same.

This means that we can begin with prayer and the experience of the spiritual in ordinary life. We can easily underestimate this: over 90 per cent of people are prepared to describe themselves as 'spiritual beings' and over 60 per cent of them pray – for some this may be a case of 'If in emergency, break glass', but others pray regularly.

Evangelism must deal with the agenda of those it addresses. Too often it begins with its own claims to truth rather than a concern for the people it addresses. For example, research shows that less than half of those who do come to faith have any sense of sin. Hence if an evangelist says 'You are a sinner', it rings no bells with them. They have no understanding that their wrongdoing is an affront to the standards of a holy God. It is too easy to respond by saying, 'They ought to feel sinful because that is their state before God.' We have to deal with people as they are, not as we would like them to be.

And what if they have no Godward agenda – if they are not needing a God who will do something for them? These are not necessarily the self-sufficient, self-centred people who are impervious to Good News. They may well want to find out about God – indeed the whole spiritual search which is typical of the 1990s can be seen in terms of a search for underlying realities rather than the 'God of repairs' which the Christian Church has too often offered: 'If you feel ashamed, we offer forgiveness'; 'If you feel confused, we offer peace of mind'; 'If you feel miserable, we offer tranquillity'. These 'free offers' are true, but a 'sticking-plaster God' is not a portrayal of all that the Godhead is. Many want to see the majesty and the reality of God and are conscious of no personal need – their search for God starts from strength rather than weakness. Their agenda does not stem from a want but from a willingness to question.

In one sense this is an intensely humanist age, and in many ways a selfish one, deeply concerned with the self and its development. Courses on self-awareness and self-knowledge proliferate and can be of value, but if they are simply to lead to greater self-fulfilment there is a need to remember the scriptural warning: 'Anyone who wants to be a follower of mine must renounce self; he must take up his cross and follow me. Whoever wants to save his life will lose it, but whoever loses his life for my sake and for the gospel's will save it'.[7]

Yet the search for identity does not have to be an introspective, self-absorbed descent into the shadows. It can be, for those who seek an answer to the questions: 'Why am I here?' 'What is the purpose of my life?' a fruitful stage in the search for truth. If the search stops with ourselves it will ultimately be barren. In its muddled way the 1990s understands this for this is not humanism as understood by the militantly atheistic Rationalist Association. People are interested in themselves, but they are also concerned with their interrelationship with the world around them, as can be seen in the multitude of environmentally friendly, socially aware attitudes which are seen as being acceptable and even fashionable. Indeed, except in its wilder fringes, political correctness seeks to be aware of and show concern for the marginalised. This has a religious dimension, as can be seen in the vast interest in the supernatural and the occult, which any self-respecting atheist would spurn with instant scorn. But it is not only this shadow side of rancid religion in which people are interested; there are many who are genuinely concerned to find themselves in relation to their Creator.

Some seek self-fulfilment as an end in itself but there are many others who perceive that it is intrinsically selfish and self-defeating and look for something deeper and wiser.

3. From missions to mission

Many peddle 'truth' from every platform – whether it is the truth about washing powders or the truth about God. People are suspicious, overwhelmed and wary of every sort of soft or hard sell. There comes a point where advertising destroys itself. If the whole world is a billboard covered with posters you eventually see none of them.

What is important is the life of the congregation. Paul recognised this when he wrote his letters to the young churches. He said hardly anything about their duty to evangelise: he said a great deal about their duty to live in wholesome unity with each other. He knew that in his day it was Christian common life which would attract attention and win converts. It is still true.

But a common life in Christ must be more than a harmonious gathering of the introverted. The 'serving community' has become a Christian cliché and is too often spoken of in theory rather than seen in practice, but the phrase describes what ought to be true of every congregation. Each church has a public face and should have work-gnarled hands.

Evangelistic events are billboard occasions when much effort is put into 'selling the gospel'. As we have seen, the 1990s are hostile to this sort of evangelism in a way which was not true even ten years ago. *Finding Faith Today* showed that only 17 per cent of those adults who had made a public profession of faith in the early 1990s said that such an occasion had been a factor (usually not the most significant) in their journey to faith.

The 1990s are sceptical of such high-profile occasions for they wish to see integrity in the church community. Post-modernism rejects me if I attempt to persuade another person to jump into my meta-narrative. Things must be discovered by people for themselves. The Church must therefore not be a community which winds itself up into a special mission every five years, but be one which *lives* mission. Mission must genuinely care for people, wanting the very best for all their lives, rather than being an attempt to cajole them into joining an organisation, even if it is the Church.

This is much more demanding of a congregation. To have an occasional mission means that a special effort only has to be cranked up every so often. To be in a position of constant service and mission means being a welcoming, open community at all times.

The importance of an open community with integrity is obvious when the results of research are taken into account. *Finding Faith Today* showed that most people come to faith through relationships. Of these 82 per cent said they had been helped by a member of their family, 61 per cent said a group of friends, 60 per cent cited a minister, 40 per cent church activities.[8]

What is a typical modern journey of faith? The details are as diverse as the number of individuals but the research showed that a frequently used pathway is:

- X is introduced into the church through a member of their family, through friendship with some Christians or through a minister;

- they begin to ask questions;

- they are invited to explore further and come to a knowledge and practice of the faith (often this is through a nurture group or some form of catechumenate);

- they discover that they have become a Christian, and mark it publicly through baptism or confirmation or whatever is appropriate to their denomination.

Professor Robin Gill sums it up when he says, 'Belonging comes before believing.'[9]

One of the most pernicious fantasies of evangelism is the reverse of this. This suggests that:

- someone encounters the gospel, usually presented through words;

- they commit their life to God;

- they look for a fellowship in which to express their new-found faith.

In reality very few find faith in this way. Most encounter the gospel within the Christian Church – and by that is not meant a church building, but the Body of Christ. Christ is encountered through people – a group of friends, a nurture group or a member of their family.

These findings take the heat out of the sterile dispute between 'churchianity' and 'Christianity'. The first is supposed to invite people to come to church and the latter to invite them to come to Christ. But in fact most people find Christ within the orbit of the Church. *Evangelism is about helping people to belong so that they can believe.*

During the 1990s there has been a massive shift from 'event-centred' to 'pastoral' evangelism. Some churches still have local missions with varying degrees of response, but much more significant are the various courses which are intended to help a group of people to discover Christ together. This has led to an interest in fairly lengthy initiatory courses from both Catholic and Evangelical stables such as various forms of catechumenates, *Alpha* courses, *Christians for Life*, *Saints Alive!* and the like. In any one year the number of people who go through these courses must be well over 200,000 – and this has to be compared with the thousands who are the best response to a mass campaign put on at great expense. Probably the greatest change in the 'New Evangelism' is the change in the typical setting of evangelism – instead of a great gathering with a speaker there is a smallish group of people seeking God together. This is not to say that big meetings no longer happen, or that the nurture group did not happen before the 1990s, but the reversal of the importance given to the two is highly significant.

These three trends are the face of 'New Evangelism'. The changes are all moving from a Roman to a Celtic model. The best modern evangelism goes where people are and listens, binds together prayer and truth, celebrates the goodness and complexity of life as well as judging the sinfulness of evil, and sees truth as something to be done and experienced as well as to be intellectually believed. It walks in humility.

This is unwelcome to those who believe in a proclamatory, arms-length style of evangelism which is dependent upon preaching a formula of salvation and a call to repentance and faith in a 'conversion experience'. The 'New Evangelism' is also questioned by those of a more liberal disposition who criticise it for being insufficiently rigorous in its intellectual search for the truth. Both conservatives and liberals would say that it is too dependent on individualistic experience of God through prayer which is not sufficiently critiqued in the light of the Bible and human reason.

These are precisely the criticisms which were made by those of a 'Roman' disposition about the Celtic Church – it was seen as too experiential, too dismissive of legal frameworks and doctrinally suspect.

Nevertheless it is an evangelism which chimes in with the post-modern world of the 1990s with its love of the fuzzy and the imprecise, its honouring of human experience and relationships and its laid-back approach to life.

The 'New Evangelism' believes in the God of orthodox Christianity and desires passionately that others should come to follow him and worship him. At the same time it is unsure of some of the proclamatory methods of the past and wishes to take seriously the changed circumstances and outlooks of the 1990s.

The old forms of evangelism will no doubt still have their place, but they are already looking curiously dated. It is with 'New Evangelism' in mind that we return to Anglo-Saxon England.

Notes

1   A phrase used by Jean-Francois Lyotard but taken further by Michael Foucault.
2   It is widely believed that this a largely Anglican affair confined to the UK. In fact it surfaced in 1988 both from the Pope and from the bishops of the Anglican Communion gathered at Lambeth, and it has been adopted by many other denominations and churches across the world. Recommendation 43 of the Lambeth Conference asked for 'a renewed and united emphasis on making Christ known to the people of his world', and Recommendation 44 asked for 'a shift to a dynamic missionary emphasis going beyond care and nurture to proclamation and service'.
3   Every one of the 27 reports produced by Anglican dioceses in the early 1990s put 'mission' alongside 'worship' as the main purposes of the Church, and cited financial constraints as the main reason the reorganisation was being done at that time. It is arguable that one of the main agents for mission in the 1990s has been the mistakes of the Church Commissioners, for this has forced the Church of England to face issues which for too long had been put on one side.

4   Cf. Peter Brierley, *Christian England* (1991). Also to be taken into account is the changing pattern of attendance – people who attend two or three Sundays a month see themselves as 'regular', and an increasing number of churches are having 'Sunday' Schools and services on weekdays because of changing patterns of work and leisure at weekends – these changes often escape the statistics.

5   *Signs of Life* (Board of Mission, 1996).

6   Cf. David Hay, *Exploring Inner Space* (2nd edn, 1987).

7   St Mark 8.34f (REB).

8   John Finney, *Finding Faith Today* (1992). From a very different angle the same point is made by David Pawson in *The Normal Christian Birth* (1989).

9   Cf. *A Vision for Growth* (1994): this should not be confused with the findings of Grace Davie in *Religion in Britain since 1945* (1994) about 'believing without belonging'. She is describing the whole population, while Gill is concerned with those who are becoming churchgoers.

Chapter 5

The Monastery in Mission

IT IS hard to rid ourselves of mental pictures of what a monastery or convent is like. We picture the ruins of the great medieval monasteries like Fountains or Rievaulx. We remember encounters with present-day monasteries with their considerable property, well-tended gardens and atmosphere of peace.

Early monasteries were not like that at all. Excavations generally show smallish separate cells, often built of wattle and daub on stone foundations. Sometimes there are interior partitions, which suggests that they were occupied by two monks. Often only the chapel and the guest house were built of stone or wood, for prayer and hospitality were two of the main purposes of the community. All the buildings were set within an enclosure, usually a hedge or dry-stone wall.

Often the communities were large and cannot have had much air of tranquillity. The Vikings boasted of destroying one monastery with 2,000 people in it – even allowing for exaggeration that suggests a considerable number of people. There would be the monks and/or nuns and a large number of others who were attached: people who gave their skills, joining in much of the life of prayer and being part of the whole community. There would have been families with children and livestock would be driven inside at nightfall. There would have been little of the monastic peace that pervades modern communities and monks went outside the enclosure when they wanted peace and quiet. Often the monasteries were the largest groups of people around, for few 'towns' had more than 300 people. As James Campbell says, 'In much of England the nearest approximation to a town was a major monastery.'

The beginning of Christian monasticism

Monasticism started in the eastern Mediterranean. The reasons for its growth are complex. In many early Christian congregations there were those who renounced marriage to give themselves to a life of prayer and service of others. By the third and fourth century we find people withdrawing from society into solitude. Some may have been fleeing persecution while, later, others were rejecting the laxity of the post-Constantinian church. There were possible precedents in the Jewish faith, where communities like the Essenes at Qumran were flourishing at the time of Christ.

Christian monasticism did not start with people living together. On the contrary it began with people seeking solitude: the very word 'monk' comes from the Greek word for 'alone'. The deserts of Egypt and Syria became dotted with hermits, some of whom were famous for their sanctity and besieged by people wanting counsel and guidance. They were austere if not masochistic in their lifestyle for, as in many religions, they denied their physical being in order to benefit their spiritual life. Their battles were internal – against 'the lusts of the world, the flesh and the devil' – especially the last. Spiritual warfare was high on the agenda, and they were revered as spiritual shocktroops in the battle against evil. Today some of their forms of holiness seem bizarre in the extreme. Macarius (d. 393) is said to have prayed without sleep, food or water for the whole of Lent; St Simeon the Stylite sat on top of his pillar for 47 years. Even such self-denial did not wholly obliterate the sin of pride, for there was clearly some competition in mortification of the flesh, with some trying to be 'more ascetic than thou'. We shall find a similar pattern in Celtic spirituality, including the tendency to exaggerate the degree of mortification.

The dots in the desert became clumps. The hermits, sometimes hundreds strong, gathered in colonies, though still keeping largely to themselves. A frequent pattern was a weekly meeting for worship led by an abbot, who was also responsible for introducing new people to the life of prayer. The hermits worked to meet their meagre needs, and even the weaving of baskets demands a simple organisation for the supply of materials and the sale of the finished product.

The hermits were laypeople – indeed they took strong exception to anyone who sought priesthood. One fifth-century writer inveighed against those who want 'clerical office out of rapid ambition . . . for their juvenile vanity they ought to be put in their place and whipped'. Jerome said, 'If you want to perform the office of a priest, live in cities and towns, and make the salvation of others the gain of your soul. But if you desire to be what is called a monk, that is a solitary, what are you doing in cities?' There was deep distrust of ecclesiastical machinery, and the advice given by Cassian says much: 'The monk should flee women and bishops'.

The clumps became communities. St Pachomius established what we would recognise as a monastery in Egypt around 320. He had been a soldier, and the rules he evolved had a military ring; even the ground plan of the monastery was not unlike that of a legionary camp. Total obedience to the superior was demanded and since some of these communities were over a thousand strong, many of them illiterate Egyptian peasants, strict discipline may have been inevitable. St Basil, greatly influenced by the Pachomian monasteries, gave them a stronger theological basis, arguing that a hermit could not fulfil Christ's command to show practical love to others – 'If you live alone, whose feet will you wash?' He also counselled against the individualism and fanaticism which had defiled some parts of the early development. Pachomius had insisted on the importance of work to keep the community viable, but it was Basil who taught that work was not just an economic necessity but a means of spiritual development.

Monks in the West

By the second half of the fourth century the monastic movement was well established and widely admired in the Greek-speaking world of the eastern Mediterranean. The *Life of St Anthony* written by Athanasius was a runaway best-seller, and when translated into Latin sparked off many imitators. The first western monks settled around Poitiers, where Hilary was bishop. He fostered the work of Martin at Tours who began his work about 360. Martin, like

Pachomius, was an ex-soldier, and after a time as an anchorite became head of a community as well as bishop, for in the West the possibility of ordained monks was not rejected as forcefully as in the East.

In Gaul a further twist in the development of monasticism took place. The Eastern monks had been distrustful of learning, seeing it as a distraction from the reading of the Scriptures and prayer. But a monastery had to be a literate society, for the daily round of worship demanded service books and Bibles and people who could read them. The Rule of the monastery and its Penitential had to be examined frequently and there would have been an accumulation of deeds and letters. As monasteries became more settled, libraries grew, filled with the writings of the church Fathers, texts needed for those being educated and biographies of the past heroes of the monastery. Monasteries with a Roman foundation had few if any of the classical writers like Ovid or Virgil, for Gregory the Great had condemned them, but the Irish monasteries had no such bar and Bede quotes freely from them. All these writings had to be copied by hand. Most would have been everyday copies, but such masterpieces as the Book of Kells or the Book of Durrow could not have been subject to such daily fingering and would have been kept for special occasions.[1] It was at Tours that the emphasis on scholarship began, and monasteries began to be places of education. It was this new element which became so important in the West that it led to the monasteries being in the forefront of learning, and it is not surprising that the early universities of Europe sprang from these monastic beginnings.

It was these converging threads of monasticism, initiated in the deserts of Egypt, enlarged in Gaul, which came to Ireland and bore much fruit.

Celtic monasticism

Legend obscures the beginning of Irish monasticism, for they were great story-tellers and the tales became more fanciful with every telling. This was the age when St Brigit (or Bridget) hung her cloak on a sunbeam and turned the Lord Mayor of London into a horse because he was rude to her. She is also claimed to be the first Irish woman priest – ordained by a short-sighted bishop!

However, we do know that when Ireland was first evangelised a normal Roman-style ecclesiastical pattern with territorial dioceses governed by bishops in their sees was established. This was in embryo when St Patrick arrived as a missionary and was reasonably well established by the time of his death in 461. The eighth-century *Catalogue of the Saints* gives this picture: 'In the time of Patrick the founders of the churches were all bishops, 350 in number, famed and holy and full of the Holy Ghost. All these bishops had come from the Romans and Britons and Scots.'

By the time of Patrick some monasteries and convents had been founded. It is generally thought that Irish monasticism was imported via Martin of Tours, for we know that there were trade links with the area – Irish shoes were imported into the Loire valley! However it is possible that some understanding of monasticism may have come direct from Egypt and Syria, for the graves of monks who originated in Egypt have been found in Ireland. Trade was well established with the eastern Mediterranean, so this is by no means fanciful. Despite the fact that Ireland was outside the Empire, considerable quantities of pottery from Syria and Egypt (mainly fragments of wine jars) made during this period have been found all over Ireland, southern Scotland and Wales.

When the mists clear in the middle of the next century an extraordinary change has taken place. It is unique in Christian history. As we have seen the dioceses disappeared and were supplanted by monasteries. Within a century the country was covered with communities. Some were large and close to populated areas, but others sought out islands and mountain tops to build their beehive-shaped stone cells.

Even more extraordinary is the change in the power structure. The most significant people now are not bishops but abbots, who were normally priests. The bishops are now part of the community and subordinate to the abbots in the hierarchy of the monastery. Thus Bede describes the organisation of Iona: 'It is always ruled by an abbot in priest's orders, to whose authority the whole province, including the bishops, is subject [Bede concludes sourly] contrary to the usual custom': i.e. the Roman pattern. As members of the community the bishops had their voice along with the rest in the choice of a new abbot, but once he was chosen they owed obedience to him. The bishops performed the sacramental actions peculiar to their order, such as ordination, but above all were the leaders of evangelistic missions into the surrounding countryside and to the local secular leadership. The strategy for evangelisation would probably have been a community decision, though obviously the bishop as evangelistic leader would have had a considerable say.

The distinction between this pattern and the Roman bishop in his see is considerable. Roman bishops could be members of a community for personal support and prayer. Hilary of Arles was one such; Gregory I retained close links with his monastery after he had become Pope; Augustine of Hippo even held that the proper lifestyle of a bishop was monastic. Nevertheless their main task was the oversight of their diocese from their cathedral. Their work was pastoral and administrative. But the Celtic bishop was the prime evangelist. When we view the disputes between the Celtic and the Roman ways which culminated in Whitby in 664 we can see that they were much more than just hairsplitting quarrels about the date of Easter – it was a clash between radically different ecclesiologies and methods of mission.

This change was not confined to Ireland. It also happened in Wales[2] and it was imported into Scotland, so becoming the normal Celtic pattern. Even more significantly, the independence of the monastery from diocesan control was seen as normal by every Celtic foundation on the mainland of Europe and brought monasteries into conflict with popes and bishops.

The reasons for this momentous change are conjectural. Some suggest that dioceses flourish best in an urban and settled society whereas Ireland did not have towns and the tribes did not have a settled homeland, but a diocesan pattern had been in place for the best part of a century before this change and bishops and dioceses flourished in other parts of Europe. It is possible that the Church was copying the pattern of the pre-Christian religious organisation in the same way that the early Church adopted much of the organisation of the Jewish synagogue. The bardic schools and the wise men attached to royal households are not far removed from the monasteries and the religious leaders working alongside the tribal chiefs. Other historians suggest that it was impossible to have a centralised authority in a social context of extreme political instability.[3] Perhaps it was the attraction of the monastic life which drew priests to it. Perhaps it was the influence of monks and others fleeing the barbarian hordes which were pouring across Europe and pushing peoples before them. Perhaps it is because only 'the Celtic fringe' kept their culture intact – because for them these were not the Dark Ages but their Golden Age. Whatever the reason monasteries became the evangelistic spearhead of the Irish Church.

It seems that market forces, not ecclesiology, were the reason for the change. In the context of Irish society the Roman pattern was unsatisfactory and so withered away because it was not a suitable means of evangelism. Conversely the monastic pattern of evangelism seems, from what we have seen in England, to have been highly effective as an evangelistic agency, and it therefore prospered.

It is easy to see ecclesiology as a dry as dust subject. But how a church is organised, what its theology of the Body of Christ is and how this is expressed is of the greatest importance for evangelism. The evangelisation of the British Isles suggests that one pattern was highly effective, the other much less so. Despite all the help which was given to the Augustinian mission from Rome and elsewhere, the homespun Celtic evangelism appears to have been far more effective.

The wanderers

One peculiarity of the Celtic monasteries were the *peregrinati* ('wanderers'). The Irish monks, like Aboriginals in Australia or native peoples in America, could not be held down. They were born wanderers. They took off for far away places. They prayed and went. Sometimes they went by sea – and found new worlds. Certainly we know that they reached Iceland, for when the Vikings discovered it some time later they found several Christian hermits living there. They promptly killed them. More speculative is the link with North America. St Brendan (c. 489–c. 578) is claimed as its first discoverer. The jury has to be out on this one. The tale describing his voyage has much of the usual fantastical phantasmagoria of such stories but also has the sense of having a basis of fact in its descriptions of icebergs and volcanoes. It is not impossible, for in 1978 Tim Severin sailed a similar boat along the route indicated in the tale and landed in North America.

But the Irish did not only wander by sea. They travelled over all of Europe and could be found as far east as Poland and the Crimea. The reason for this wandering was the usual mixture of motives which govern most of human activity. The Irish themselves recognised that there was a racial restlessness that led them to go walkabout, and they sought to purify that wanderlust. Some wanted to venture far for Christ. The story is told of the three monks who got into a coracle on the south coast of Ireland but took no oars. They drifted over to Cornwall. Brought before King Alfred they disingenuously explained, 'We stole away because we wanted for the love of God to be on pilgrimage, we care not where.' If the medieval Book of Lismore is to be believed the early Celts saw three kinds of pilgrimage. The first pilgrims were merely wandering and wasting their time. The second group were those who wanted to go on pilgrimage but could not, because of responsibilities at home. The third, and most highly regarded, were those who left their country for God.

The sixth-century traveller had to travel light. You could take little with you on your back or in a coracle and this chimed in well with a spirituality which saw austerity as a means of coming closer to God. The very hardships and dangers of the journey could be offered to God. At the same time we should not exaggerate the difficulties. There was a surprising amount of travelling in this period despite the time needed and the dangers inherent in moving across unstable societies. Benedict Biscop travelled the 3,000-miles round trip from Northumbria to Rome five times in his life.

Whatever the motives, the *peregrinati* enabled the Celtic monastic movement to move fast and far. They often travelled in groups. Where they stopped they evangelised and maintained as far as possible their monastic life of prayer and contemplation. If their mission to the area bore fruit they would settle and a new monastery would be born. The process can be most easily seen in the Columbanian communities of Northern Gaul. The first settlement at Annegray was followed by widespread evangelism in the region. This led to further settlements at Fontaine and

Luxeuil and from there they soon dotted their communities over all of Gaul. Some like Luxeuil were large communities, but there must have been many others where only a few brothers or sisters lived a common life in humble dwellings. When his comments about the sexual habits of the royal household led to an enforced pilgrimage, Columbanus and his companions went into Switzerland and Italy. But it was only in part a forced departure. Columbanus had already wanted to be on the move. He had his eye upon a mission to the Slavs far to the east; he never reached his goal but, like St Paul with his longing to reach Spain, he achieved much in the journey. It is because of the need to wander that we find Celtic monks turning up all over England. Cedd (d. 664) began as a monk in Lindisfarne. He then went with his brother into the Midlands when Penda allowed evangelistic work there, and later still he evangelised Essex where he founded churches at Bradbury and Tilbury. We finally find him again in the north establishing a monastery at Lastingham in North Yorkshire. As Kathleen Hughes says: 'Monasticism was the perfect flexible instrument to accommodate the Irish love of wandering.'

These people had their eye on the horizon. It made them difficult to live with, and there are stories of communities composed of both Irish and English monks being split by the disgruntlement of the English at the habit of their brethren departing on a pilgrimage, especially during the better weather when there was work to be done.

The *peregrinati* did not meet with favour in the Roman system and the Benedictine Rule. The Synod of Hertford (672) had no less than three of its ten 'chapters' dealing with the matter. It categorically stated that 'monks shall not wander from place to place ... except with letter dismissory from their own abbot'. It is clear that the *peregrinati*'s example had been catching, for the secular clergy were commanded not to 'wander about at will' nor to 'exercise any priestly function without permission from the bishop in whose diocese they were'. It has a curiously modern ring, for it is a question which has been raised in a few cases of church-planting today, where congregations have been started without permission from the diocesan bishop.

Double monasteries

One other peculiarity of Celtic monasticism were the double monasteries where both monks and nuns lived in one community. Their living quarters were apart and they normally came together only for worship, but they were subject to only one person. Convents have always needed a few priests nearby to take care of the sacramental side of their life, but the Celts had communities of which half were monks and half nuns.

There was no reason why the person in charge of a double community should not be a woman. The most famous case is Hilda of Whitby, who had both priests and bishops under her authority. The beginning of this pattern is probably to be found in Gaul, where the Columbanian convents had acquired larger groups of priests than normal – but always under the leadership of the abbess. From Gaul they spread into England – but not to Ireland – further evidence of the evangelisation of England from the Irish foundations in continental Europe.

Abbesses were formidable women. Like Hilda they were usually of royal birth, for kings had begun to send their spare daughters off to convents and they expected to be treated as their lineage demanded. They were imperious characters. Their nuns and monks were so much in awe of them that they thought that even death did not loosen their hold. The story is told that ten years after the death of Gertrude of Nivelles fire broke out in the convent and the nuns helplessly cowered together to watch it burn to the ground. Suddenly on the top of the refectory roof they saw a familiar figure beating back the flames with her veil and saving the buildings.

Celtic attitudes to women seem to have been different to those which stemmed from either Rome or the Anglo-Saxons and we shall need to look at this more carefully, not least because some have claimed that the Celts were the first 'politically correct' peoples in the world. However, it can be noted that these 'royal personages' had very great authority and wielded it vigorously. They did not hesitate to trespass on the normal preserves of the priesthood, and in the Celtic monasteries abbesses heard confessions and absolved the penitent.

As far as the Romans were concerned this was another of the

detestable practices of the Celtic Church. Archbishop Theodore (d. 690) disapproved of it and gradually the double houses decayed.

Celtic and Roman learning

The place of education in the monastic tradition is by no means confined to the Celtic Church. Schools were set up in Kent immediately after the arrival of Augustine and King's School, Canterbury claims to have been founded in 604, only nine years after the first landing. By 700 Tobias of Rochester could be said to be 'a scholar of Latin, Greek and Saxon'. The mention of Saxon is significant – already people were beginning to value the vernacular and the small library of Anglo-Saxon writings was growing.

However, this did not compare with what was happening in the west and north. Roman education was primarily for the young and 'clarity of expression was a special Roman virtue'.[4] However, the Celtic emphasis was different from the Roman: where the Romans taught children, the Celts taught adults as well.

The Celts had always had a reputation for learning – the pagan bards had an educational element in their work despite their prohibition of writing. Once writing began with the conversion to Christianity in the sixth century there was a flowering of literature. Indeed Calvert Watkins of Harvard claims that it is 'the oldest vernacular literature in Europe'. This was particularly true of the Welsh, and in the sixth century the love of learning spread into Ireland, especially from Llantwit Major in Glamorgan. Where the Romans stressed order and clarity, the Celts loved poetry and revelled in colour and design. At its best Celtic literature is still readable and delightful, at its worst it is over-elaborate and obscure with too frequent use of bizarre words.

The three streams of Celtic, Roman and Saxon flowed together in the extraordinary outburst of creativity and scholarship centred in Northumbria in the late seventh century. The Book of Durrow was written in an Irish monastery, used the Roman Vulgate and is decorated with patterns which are immediately reminiscent of the jewellery from the Anglo-Saxon Sutton Hoo ship-burial.

From the Roman tradition came the libraries and the discipline of scholarship. Benedict Biscop scoured Europe and 'brought back a large number of books on all branches of sacred knowledge, some bought at a favourable price, others the gifts of well-wishers'.[5] Bede quotes from over 100 authors, by no means all of them Christians: books on science and by pagan writers like Virgil and Pliny were well known to him.

The Celtic tradition lightened the rather heavy Roman pattern. In the manuscripts the austere but serviceable Roman letters are touched by a Celtic extravagance of design and the bold use of colour. Small animals peep out between the entwinings and the abundance of the natural forms envelops the straightforward form of the letter. Exuberance and delight in artistic creation can be seen on every illuminated page.

Poetry was close to the heart of the Celt and verse was the usual form of writing in an age when the need to memorise was often more important than the need to read. Allied to this were the books of hagiography which told improving stories of the saints of old. One wonders if even the writers believed that these tales had any historical basis.

We have less evidence of the Saxon stream of learning, but the magnificence of the craftsmanship of the Sutton Hoo burial reminds us that the Anglo-Saxons were not savages. Their ability to work wood and metal and their decorative skills were remarkable and they brought with them the precious gift of a language which was just beginning, which could be moulded and developed more easily than the mature Latin of the Romans.

The Celtic monasteries are probably best remembered today for the extraordinary manuscripts which have survived. To see the Book of Kells, vivid and beautiful even now, is to see into the Celtic world. Cassiodorus had founded two monasteries near Rome in about 540, and these became famous for the copying of biblical manuscripts, for he held that every word of Scripture that he wrote 'was a wound inflicted on Satan'. It is the copies of the Bible which made the Northumbrian and Irish Church famous throughout the contemporary world, and the Celtic invention of half-uncial writing was both admired and copied. Indeed many of the finest English manuscripts that remain are on the continent because so many in England were destroyed by the Vikings. They were of fabulous value even in their day. The three manuscripts which we know were written at Jarrow/Monkwearmouth would have taken 1,550 calfskins, and the gold and precious colours were costly and rare. The Codex Amiatinus has 2,060 pages and weighs more than half a hundredweight. Taking into account the endless hours of work which each manuscript represented, it is not difficult to see why they were so highly prized.

In the excavations at Whitby many styli have been unearthed. Held in frozen hands they produced magnificence. But the grumbles they wrote in the margins reveal the human cost. 'Twenty days to Easter Monday and I am cold and tired.' 'Do not reproach me concerning the letters: the ink is bad, the parchment scanty, the day dark.'

The organisation of Celtic monasteries

Every grouping of people, even a Celtic one, has to have a framework in which to operate. The way a monastery or convent was governed determined its potentiality. It was expected that most of the monks and nuns would live communally, though some of them would be hermits, only loosely attached to the mother house.

The Celtic monastery with the abbot as its head and the bishops as evangelists was a fine vehicle for mission. The bishops led teams out to evangelise and they came back to the monastery for refreshment and renewal. Columbanus, despite his peripatetic life used to return for 50-day retreats of complete solitude with God.

It was Columbanus who produced the best known Rule in the Celtic churches for his far-flung monasteries on the continent. Immediately we are struck by its inhumanity: 'Let the monk come weary and as if sleep-walking to his bed, and let him be forced to rise while his sleep is not yet finished . . . Let him fear the superior of his community as a lord.' Breaking the rule of silence at meals was punished with six lashes; smiling during services, six lashes; contradicting the words of someone else, fifty lashes. Amazingly, people flocked to join the Columbanian monasteries.

In the Celtic monasteries the abbot was supreme. He – or she – made the decisions autocratically. Even more importantly they chose their successor. For a fast-moving missionary situation this had its advantages, but again we find that the Celtic pattern was excellent for mission but not suited for a more settled situation.

Where there was a wise and evangelistically orientated abbot all was well, but when the love of the institution took over, there were grave opportunities of abuse. The Benedictine Rule of the Roman Church was more adapted to the long-term good of the monastery but changed it from being a mission station to a settled institution. It can be argued that the Benedictine Rule cannot be mission-centred: time and again down the centuries communities have been established with an evangelistic aim, but within a couple of generations they have become institutionalised and introverted.

This Celtic autocratic rule became a matter of the greatest conse-quence when social status and money began to be important. Many of the early abbots and abbesses had royal blood, and many of them were outstanding people by any standards. But they were people of their age and when choosing their successors they did not want to lower the tone by appointing a commoner. Among the Celts kinship was important and they often appointed a member of their own family – who may well not have had the wisdom and spiritual depth required. A contemporary warned, 'An abbess ought to be noble in wisdom and in holiness, as well as noble by birth.'⁶ The Benedictine Rule was less concerned to 'keep it in the family': Benedict Biscop, a fervent follower of Roman ways in his latter years, warned on his deathbed, 'I would far rather have the monastery revert to a wilderness than have my brother, who has not entered on the way of truth, succeed me as abbot.' This social consciousness was compounded by the developing practice of allowing religious foundations exemption from taxes and service to the king. There were undoubtedly cases where the setting up of a monastery became a tax dodge where part of a rich man's estate could, by a legal fiction, be made over to a monastery and enjoy its financial advantages when in reality the monastery remained part of his property. There were even cases of whole families deciding to devote themselves to the religious life, take vows and build a church; sometimes this was for genuine love of God but sometimes it could be a way out of onerous obligations. Under Germanic law a monastery was presumed to belong to its founder and, in the wrong hands, this could be too easily exploited.

As people became Christian so they were grateful for the work of the mission teams who had brought them to faith. They heaped riches upon the monasteries – which began to decay. Even by Bede's time this process was happening: he complained bitterly about the loss of the simple lifestyle and rigorous spiritual life of the early saints and missionaries. Aldhelm (639–709) mentions a golden chalice encrusted with gems, and even St Cuthbert (c. 634–687) left beautiful things behind him, including the fine pectoral cross still to be seen at Durham.

It is not surprising that by the time the Vikings came in the ninth century and swept many of them away, those monastic foundations which were still dependent upon a Celtic pattern of government were already rotten from within.

The Benedictine Rule

A *Life* of Gregory I written in Whitby portrayed him as the great apostle of England, who at the Day of Judgement would lead the whole English nation before the Lord. Certainly he had a pivotal role in the evangelisation of England because of the sending of the Italian missionaries. As we have seen, this achieved less than was once thought, but Gregory may have had an indirect impact which was greater and lasted longer. In 593, while he was Pope, he found the time to write the *Dialogues*. The second part of this was a hagiography of a rather obscure abbot called Benedict. Benedict had died forty years before, after founding a monastery at Monte Cassino. In passing Gregory mentions that Benedict had written a Rule for his monks, 'remarkable for its discretion and the lucidity of its language'. The *Dialogues* greatly influenced the contemporary church and was popular for long afterwards, and publicised Benedict and his achievements.

The Rule was not all Benedict's own work. It drew together 'good practice' from different sources and expressed it in straightforward language. While Gregory's backing had a considerable effect, the Rule established itself, over against the considerable number of alternatives, by its commonsense approach to the monastic life. The Rule had the force of law, and abbots were not allowed to modify it. It caught the tide, for this was an age of codification as Europe began to struggle back to normality after the barbarian incursions, and at Constantinople Justinian was drawing together his *Institutes*, the great epitome of Roman law.

Now, instead of each community making its own Rule with the inevitable mistakes, a commonly accepted standard for all monasteries could be adopted.

In the Rule of St Benedict the abbot is all-important, but his rule is less autocratic than in the Celtic monasteries, and in his decisions he must listen to the opinion of the whole community, down to the newest novice. Further he is elected by his brethren, rather than being able to appoint his successor, as was common practice elsewhere, including the Celtic foundations.

It is expected that there will be solitaries attached loosely to the monastery but they must not be those 'in the first fervour of the ascetical life'. The hermits were to be those who were spiritually mature, not those driven by a desire to be admired as true 'soldiers of Christ'.

Benedict did not approve of the Celtic *peregrinati*. Indeed he called them *gyrovagi* ('gadabouts') 'concerning whose miserable way of life it is better to be silent than to speak', for those he had come across were not venturing for Christ but spongers going from monastery to monastery abusing their hospitality.

When the Columbanian and Benedictine Rules came into contact in Gaul a mixed economy grew up. Not surprisingly the less severe Benedictine punishments for misdemeanours were preferred to those of Columbanus, but other Celtic elements continued for a long time, until the pure Benedictine form became the norm.

In England monasteries adopted the Benedictine Rule. Some did it enthusiastically like Wilfred at Ripon, but most did so with reluctance, and it would be centuries before the old Celtic patterns were totally overlaid by the Benedictine.

It is difficult to be sure of the number of monastic foundations in England. Augustine only founded one monastery, at Canterbury. However, the Celtic communities seem to have been very much more thickly scattered and by Bede's death they had become numerous. Many of them would have been modest affairs of which we have no record, but in the Worcester area we have better evidence and we know of 32 foundations in the immediate vicinity of the city. If that density was true across the country there would have been many thousands.

In many cases they would have pastored only a small area and fulfilled the role of the parish priest, tending the sick, providing the sacraments, keeping the round of prayer and vigil. Before long the two systems merged – the old missionary urge had gone and the settled parochial system had arrived.

Today – mission and movement

The rapid spread and effectiveness of the Irish monasteries in the sixth, seventh and eighth centuries depended on elements which can speak to us today despite the cultural gulf between them and us. They were 'planting' monasteries, and can illustrate the possibilities and problems of church-planting.

Movement

The Celts saw movement as of the essence of the gospel. Their travels may have been partly due to an innate wanderlust or a social context which was less rooted in geography than in tribal loyalties, but there was a basic understanding that evangelism is linked with a thrust from an area of safety into a potentially dangerous world. Today's church often wants mission without movement, and it becomes no more than a polite request to the world to come and hear the gospel. When the world just as politely declines, the church is nonplussed and wrings its hands over human obduracy.

In recent years 'church-planting' has become fashionable. It describes the process whereby a group of people attempt to found a new church. Most of these groups have come from a single 'mother church', though there have been a few instances when those involved have been drawn from several churches, or even different denominations. The strength of the idea is that it sees mission as movement. It incarnates the gospel by identifying with a geographical area, for usually a church plant is founded in a particular area and tries to serve the people there. But this does not always have to be true. There have been examples when churches have been founded in a non-geographical context usually within a certain culture. Often this has been the youth culture, so that the church identifies with the needs of youth, accepting the way they react and worshipping in a style they can relate to. The difficulties associated with the 'Nine O'Clock Service' in Sheffield should not condemn this evangelism. It is inevitably 'on the edge', for it is identifying with a culture where drugs and sex without commitment are as popular as ecological awareness and generosity to the needs of the poor. But this 'tribal church-planting' does not have to be confined to young people. One church was formed by pensioners: they took the initiative when they found no nearby church which could cater for their needs, and they formed one of the most rapidly growing churches in the neighbourhood. The Celtic monks were engaged in the same process in their 'monastery-planting' for they too sought to establish a vibrant Christian community of prayer and service.

Community

Irish monks seldom travelled alone. Three went to Cornwall, twelve went with Columba to Iona and a sizeable group with Columbanus. Each group was a community on the move. The importance of this is once again illustrated by church-planting. New churches have, of course, been planted before: even the oldest in the land was founded at some time in the past. But nearly all have been established by one person or one family. In Anglican history this has typically been a priest alone or accompanied by his wife. In the Methodist and Baptist past one family has often been the founders. Evangelism in non-Christian countries has often been pioneered by a single missionary, frequently at great personal cost. Both the Celts and the church-planters believe in the importance of the team. A group of people can pray and think together. They inspire and encourage each other. The single entrepreneur is too easily prey to self doubt and loss of vision. The 'Elijah syndrome' of depression and self-pity can become predominant. On Mount Carmel, Elijah poured out his woes to God: 'I, I only am left, and they seek my life to take it away.' God's response to Elijah was suitably robust: 'There are still seven thousand in Israel who have not bowed their knee to Baal.' He was no longer to be a lone ranger, but should join the rest of the team, and for the remainder of his ministry he was given the companionship of Elisha. The church-planting team need people with gifts appropriate to the situation: at the very least they need a pastor to care for people, a teacher to help people to understand the faith, an evangelist to help them them into faith and an administrator to make sure it all runs smoothly.

Discipline and prayer

The Celtic team were centred on discipline and prayer. When they settled in an area they carried on the regime of prayer which they brought from their home monastery: the offices were recited and the Scriptures were studied. If a priest was present they celebrated the eucharist. A Christian colony was established and drew in people from the neighbourhood. The church-planting movement needs to learn from this. A planting team will need a mutual commitment of prayer together. Probably they cannot live together as closely as the celibate Irish monks but there should be some form of 'Third Order'.[7] Time and again it was the quality of life of the monks which drew others to their community, moved the hearts of kings and opened doors for new work.

Lay initiatives

Both the Irish monks and the typical modern church-planting team are mainly lay initiatives. There may or may not be priests in the team, but they are certainly not essential to the enterprise. The Irish monks had inherited the typical Eastern suspicion of those who were ordained and, although this was relaxed so that eventually both priests and bishops were accepted as part of the monastic community, the great majority would have been lay. On the whole laypeople relate more easily to laypeople and a newly established monastery would have been a working community. In their home monastery they would have been carpenters, builders, farmers and potters and so when they settled in a new area they would naturally have followed their old trades.

We can imagine such a group coming into a village. If they were kindly received they would build a hut on a patch of spare land. They would have slipped into the routine of village life, using their skills, possibly clearing the scrub and hacking out new farming land from the nearby forest. If they continued to prosper, the old hut would be discarded for a more permanent building on the cleared land and the first church might be attached to it. One of the team might be chosen as the first abbot and more formal services begin. There is evidence of this happening and it is a natural progression. However, as soon as the monastery became too settled a group of monks would ask the abbot if they could go a-wandering and the process would begin again. Sometimes it appears to have been haphazard and dependent upon the whim of the individual monk. At other times, as in a Columbanian mission, it appears to have been a deliberate policy to plant new monasteries as fast as possible. Planned or unplanned, monasteries multiplied at an astonishing rate – as we have seen, one small area could have 32 monasteries established within half a century.

Dangers

There were dangers. A community could be self-serving, with a group of disobedient monks leaving a monastery to set up a rival body. At other times it could be a pleasant wander through the summer months partially free from the discipline of the monastery, pleasing themselves, as the English monks complained when linked with the Irish. But the gains of the Irish missions were far greater than the dangers. There was some control on the wanderers: they were not fancy-free. Although physically absent from the home monastery they were still under its discipline. They could be, and were, summoned back to explain what they were doing. In extreme cases their new monastery could be closed, for the monasteries were all linked under a common discipline.

The Roman monasteries saw the risks as being greater than the gain. We have already seen the stricture of Benedict upon the *gyrovagi*, and the demand that monks should stay at home. But the Celts were prepared to risk it and in the light of history it looks as though they were right. The *peregrinati*, although they presumably had the usual human mixture of motives, were highly evangelistic. The Benedictine monasteries spread far more slowly and were less determined to take the gospel to the heathen. The Benedictine Order is not primarily evangelistic, despite efforts which have been made from time to time – that has been left to the Franciscans and others. Exactly the same criticisms about lack of accountability have been made of the church-planting movement. What is to prevent each new 'plant' from becoming diseased through heresy, or divided because of rivalry between leaders or sin in the church? Exactly the same problems are mentioned by St Paul in references to the churches he planted in Asia Minor and Greece. It is no more possible to guarantee that these things will not happen in modern situations than for Paul to prevent them happening in Corinth or Galatia. It is a risk worth taking, particularly if a suitable system of oversight (*episcope*) can be put in place. For the Irish, it was the links with their home monastery and the following of a common Rule. For modern church-planters there are other possible sources of accountability. First there is the link which should continue with the mother church and its accumulated wisdom. While the sending church should not control the new group, it can and should offer advice and prayer. Second there will be some denominational links, which should not be tossed ungratefully aside. This may be a superintendent, a bishop or a synod of presbyters. They are often feared by venturesome church-planters as possible negative forces, and sometimes they are, for they can be over-cautious, frightened of 'setting a precedent' and niggly about church law. But that seems to be exceptional. Of recent church plants in the Church of England 99 per cent have been done with the approval, and often the active assistance of the bishop and diocesan authorities, as is detailed in the official Church of England Report *Breaking New Ground* (1994). The Report was produced for the House of Bishops because of unease about one or two highly public cases when church plants appeared to ignore or flout normal courtesies. The conclusion was reassuring.[8]

It can be said that the Benedictine reaction to *gyrovagi* is the attitude of a 'safety first' church, concerned mainly about the preservation of its own life and more conscious of dangers than of opportunities. Behind the fear is an unwillingness to trust individuals to make decisions and bear the consequences. This basic lack of trust (and the handing over of responsibility which goes with it) has hamstrung too much of the modern church. It has set in place a series of checks and balances, of committees and synods and voting methods which ensure that no one tradition can be dominant and all can be consulted and involved in any decision. The negative side of this is that any decision which is made takes so long to be completed and is so emasculated in the process that it is hardly worth making. It is better to take risks and correct people if responsibility is misused, than to be risk-free and achieve nothing. In the large committees beloved by many churches, the lack of trust is evident: nearly always it is a small caucus who propose new ideas, make the decisions and eventually act upon them, if their proposal has survived the gruelling journey through agendas and minutes, points of order and amendments to amendments. Ideas strike out bravely but shrink in the committee. Seldom do creative suggestions come from a committee – all too often it can only polish a proposal and turn quickly to the next business; at best they pray for it and encourage it forward. On the other hand, the force of a small group of enthusiasts who are knowledgeable about their subject is considerable and it is often wise to trust them – on the understanding that they take responsibility for failure as well as praise for success. It is noticeable that the churches in Africa and Asia are less encumbered by these carefully balanced structures and are more prepared to take risks; it may explain their explosive growth in some areas. It may also account for a generally more autocratic style of leadership in many of these churches, since there is more need for discipline if things go wrong. Accountability there must be, but it is better given to an individual rather than to a committee.

Sense of adventure
The Celtic monks had another element sadly lacking in the modern church – a sense of adventure. While many become Christians because of the security there is in Christ, and many within the church seek nothing more than a homely dullness, there are many others who long to take risks for Christ. Both young and old need the opportunity to be *peregrinati* – to venture new things for Christ. They may achieve much or nothing. They may be hurt or helped in the attempt, but whatever happens they will have grown in knowing the ways of God, discovering themselves as people and adding to their store of experience.

At present opportunities of adventure are seen outside the routine life of the churches. Whether it is young people going round the world with Operation Mobilization, undertaking relief work in Africa, evangelising dangerously, the need is clear: many of us need to walk near the edge of the cliff. I met a group of five young Anglicans who had taken what many would regard as a surprisingly fundamentalist view of Luke 10. They had set out to evangelise in East Anglia, and they had taken 'neither purse nor scrip' and relied upon God to support them during the ten days of their mission. They reported to me that they had never lacked a bed nor a meal. On one occasion they had been walking hungrily along a road when a woman approached them with five parcels – she was not a churchgoer but she had 'felt' that she should get ready five packets of sandwiches.

Education

Irish and Roman missionaries used a form of evangelism which is not often attempted these days in the western world, though it is more common where there is still a strong sense of community, as in parts of Asia and Africa. In a mass baptism there were inevitably those who were bemused, those who barely knew what was happening as well as those who gave a heartfelt 'Yes' to Christ. The missionaries sought to baptise them into a society which was being Christianised. To demonstrate the powerlessness of the pagan gods they destroyed their images, but they kept the temples and turned them into churches. They took the old pagan feasts and baptised them into Christ, often in a fairly perfunctory manner: like a film exposed twice when a second photo is superimposed on the first, both are still to be seen. But the missionaries went beyond this superficial change: they began to educate. Initially through preaching and verbal communication, and later through schools and the wider introduction of writing and reading, people were taught the faith. By the end of the seventh century it was expected that monks would be able to read and write, both for lections in the conduct of public worship and for private reading. In Monkswearmouth each monk was allowed to borrow one of the precious manuscripts each year and was expected to master it during that time. Study became part of the life of the monastery and it led to the magnificence of scholarship seen supremely in Northumbria but by no means confined there. Soon children began to be taught in monasteries and convents. At first they were the offspring of royalty and the nobility, like the princesses who were sent over to France in the way young Englishwomen used to be sent to a Continental finishing school. It brought them in touch with a more sophisticated wisdom as well as teachers in the main subjects of the day. However, even in the early days, it was not confined to the aristocracy. Promising boys and girls would be taken into the monastery at an early age and educated. Bede himself was taken to Jarrow as a boy of seven.

The public realm was also evangelised. Only six years after

Augustine came, the laws of Kent were codified in a Roman pattern and similar laws were soon enacted to give a special place to the Christian faith and the life of the Church. From then on the exhortations of the missionaries were backed by the force of the state, and subjects of the king were expected to conform. As the old Roman ways seeped back into England after their long absence we need to remember that they had been changed, for they were those of the new Christian Rome, not the semi-pagan Rome of the fourth century.

This kind of evangelism which seeks to convert whole communities is seldom practised today. There have been attempts to evangelise the public realm made by Christians commenting on current issues, and there have been deeper attempts to change the attitudes of public debates through the 'Gospel and our Culture' movement. But the Christianising of a whole community is attempted only through Christian schools, and the evidence is that they have only a very limited effect.

More realistic is the evangelisation of the family. Too often we accept the individualisation which is so much part of modern thinking and we evangelise individuals, often forgetful of their social setting. Our evangelism of the family has been poor. The Church provides little in the way of the family 'rites' which are such a mainstay of the Jewish faith, and offers little help to parents on the upbringing of their children and little on how to bring a whole family to Christ. Much work needs to be done on this.

Notes

1   In fact the lack of cross references in the Book of Kells would have made it extraordinarily difficult to use.

2   Very probably introduced by Irish immigrants. 'It is by no means improbable that during the fifth and sixth centuries the sum total of Irish settlers and their families in western Britain equalled or even exceeded that of the various Germanic tribes' (James Campbell, *Essays in Anglo-Saxon History* (1986).

3   See James Wilson, *Christian Theology and Old English Poetry* – though dioceses had been sources of strength at the time of the barbarian invasion of Europe, and Ireland was peaceful compared with the continent.

4   H. R. Lyon, *Anglo-Saxon England and the Norman Conquest* (1991).

5   Bede, *Lives of the Abbots*. Benedict Biscop was trying to make Monkwearmouth and Jarrow show places for the Roman practices which he was introducing. Therefore he did not only bring books: he brought relics,

ornaments, vestments, icons. To build the monasteries he also brought masons and glaziers and people to make mortar – skills which had died out with the departure of the Romans. In one spectacular coup he also persuaded John, the chief cantor at St Peter's in Rome, to come to Northumbria to teach the right way to sing. In an age when music could not be written down, the office of the cantor was essential for seemly worship in the Roman style that he was trying to introduce.

6   Walter of Luxeuil, *Rule for a Father of Virgins*.

7   A group of people attached to a religious foundation who work, bring up family, move house etc. but maintain a constant Rule of prayer and study – mainly by themselves, but together when possible. The Franciscan Third Order is probably the best known.

8   This represents the most thorough appraisal of church-planting by any denomination in the UK. Something of a church-planting bandwagon is in evidence – conferences, seminars and committees. The danger is that 'when all is said and done, much was said and little was done'.

Chapter 6

Culture Clash

WHAT DO the people next door think about? What are their attitudes, their prejudices, their enthusiasms? Do they have faith in anything – or anyone? In other words, what makes them tick?

No church should begin to engage in ministry and mission unless it is aware of people's belief patterns. The debate on 'The Gospel and Culture', largely inspired by Bishop Lesslie Newbigin, has opened up the whole subject. For myself I find the discussion exciting and positive, but I wonder if it engages with the complexities of the subject. Most of its attack is upon the Enlightenment and the modernism which has followed it. But, as we have seen in Chapter 4, modernism is itself being supplanted by postmodernism.

Further, the assumption is sometimes made in the debate that we inhabit only one culture. But we are in fact enmeshed in many. We live in a much more pluriform society than is often allowed for. Every one of us inhabits many cultures: they encircle us and influence deeply all we do and say.

Mega-culture

There are at least three levels of culture that we experience. The first is the 'mega-culture' – one overarching construct which North Americans and Europeans can describe as 'western civilisation'. It is said that its springs are in the Enlightenment with its individualism, determinism and inability to take seriously anything which cannot be measured. The Church is right to resist the corrosive effects of this, even if rather late in the day. Unfortunately, just as armies are often trained to fight the last war rather than the next, the Church is apt to fight the last battle rather than the one that needs to be fought now. We now live in a post-modern world where Enlightenment values and mores are increasingly questioned. The extreme individualism represented by Thatcherism, which is very much a product of Enlightenment thinking, is giving way to a surrender to communitarianism. Instead of ignoring emotions and relationships, people are now almost obsessively 'getting in touch with their feelings'. The excessive dependence on the rational is giving way to a dangerous surrender to the irrational, as can be seen by the growth of fundamentalism and much New Age thinking.

The New Age phenomenon is indicative of this. Probably only 40–80,000 people regularly take part in organised New Age groups and there are reported to be 1,600 of these groups in the UK at present.[1] In other words there are a large number of groups with comparatively few people in each. The occasional big group which swims to the surface of media attention is the exception rather than the rule. However, despite these limited numbers, the effect of New Age thinking has been pervasive in subjects as diverse as women's fashion and the way in which science is viewed. It is curious that in an age when astronomy and space exploration are showing us a universe so strange and so wonderful as to entrance even the most earthbound, many people are turning away to such irrational byproducts as astrology and the search for little green men.[2]

We are at the beginning of a new way in which human beings in the West view the world. What sort of world-view will emerge is not yet clear. The Church must make its contribution, seeing it as an exciting liberation from the constrictions of the Enlightenment which have been deeply corrosive of the heart of the Church, rather than something to be resisted. Whether or not the Christian Church makes its contribution, other religions and other 'isms' will certainly make theirs.

Midi-cultures

But we inhabit other cultures besides the mega-culture. It is these 'midi-cultures' which determine the sort of television programme we watch, the clothes we buy, the sort of shop we use, even the names we give our children. Advertisers sometimes know us better than we know ourselves.

The most obvious midi-cultures are our nationhood, our social class, our gender, our education.

The country where we were born determines for most of us the language we speak, the loyalties we have and the prejudices we inherit. Even if we have rebelled against the straitjacket and refused to accept it as the norm for ourselves, it is that background we have rebelled against. We may be English and rebel against the insularity which we think this engenders – but we rebel against Englishness: we cannot rebel against Frenchness because we are not French.

Our social class determines the parameters in which we feel comfortable. The way in which we are 'expected' to behave, what is forbidden and what is encouraged, determines much of how we react to events. From the trivia of table manners to the sort of job we expect to get, we have been given a framework. It can be both useful and constricting. Some people are able to step over social boundaries fairly easily; others gird against their upbringing and surroundings but they are still strongly influenced by them.

Our gender is another midi-culture. We need not decide here whether the differences between the sexes are caused by nurture or by genetic inheritance, but differences there are, and our outlook and reactions are coloured by them.

Our education defines for us another midi-culture. Whether we are well-educated or ill-educated, whether we are innately intelligent or not, leads to another set of fences within which we lead our lives.

These midi-cultures are not static. Like our mega-culture they are changing even while we live within them. Europeans are having their nationhood reshaped within the European Community; social class is being redefined by economic pressures; the alteration in gender expectations is discussed in every magazine; education has changed radically under Thatcherite policies. Midi-cultures are in a ferment.

Mini-cultures

The same is true of 'mini-cultures'. Traditionally the most significant of these are family and local community. The sort of home
we grew up in and the one we now inhabit mould us. Similarly
our neighbourhood enables us or traps us. (Today we might well
add that we are shaped by our shopping and our transport. The
sort of place we shop and the availability of transport play a
considerable part in the attitudes we have and the way we behave.)

These mini-cultures are also being transfigured. A third of
children are born 'out of wedlock', cohabitation is normal, few
neighbourhoods do not change in radical ways in a couple of
generations.

Mega-, midi- or mini-?

It is this interaction of the many different cultures which we
inhabit which largely determines the sort of people we are. All of
them are changing. They are not different fixed compartments like
the coaches on a train which we visit one by one. Rather they are
like gases intermingling and changing their composition. They
are indeed the air we breathe.

The faith community

Where does our faith come in? Is our faith and our church community mega-, midi-, or mini? The answer has to be that it is any
or all of them. For some people faith is a mini-culture: like belonging to a gardening club, church is important in a limited way but
their faith does not impinge upon much of life. Interestingly, we
find that mini-cultures may affect other mini-cultures but seldom
midi- or mega-cultures. Hence this level of faith may affect our
attitude to our family, and our immediate community may well
be influenced by our churchgoing and our prayer. However it will
not affect the way in which we approach our midi- or mega-
cultures. Our basic lifestyle is not changed.

For a smaller number of people faith is also a midi-culture.
Faith permeates and alters their thinking about their nationality,
their class, their gender, their education. Churchgoing is the
entrance into a faith community which challenges the way they

vote, their attitude to moral issues, their treatment of other people. These are the people who 'bring faith into politics', to the bemusement and sometimes anger of those who see faith only as belonging to the private mini-culture sphere of life.

For a still smaller number faith is not peripheral – it is a mega-culture supreme over all other factors. If the prevailing secular mega-culture collides with the faith culture then it is the former which has to give way. For those people their faith is the bedrock on which they found their lives and all else seems merely the swirl of temporary fashion.

There is no doubt that the New Testament expects the last: faith in God through the person of Jesus Christ and the infilling of the Holy Spirit should be paramount over all other claims upon a believer's life. There is also no doubt that few people attain it within the Christian faith, for it should be immediately apparent in a radical change in lifestyle, and simple observation shows that this happens to few. The Christian faith is itself a mega-culture and the New Testament is the story of a new mega-culture coming into contact and conflict with the prevailing one. Like tectonic plates colliding there is much heat generated at the boundary. The New Testament shows the effect of the encounter with the Roman government and the prevailing Jewish faith through the men and women 'who have turned the world upside down'.

There is one exception to the inevitability of this collision. When the secular mega-culture is so permeated by Christianity that they merge into each other then the likelihood of major disruption recedes. Possibilities of conflict remain but they are contained and local. This is the model of 'Christendom' which we have inherited; it has dominated the western world for the past thousand years and more and is now breaking apart with loud cracking noises. Christendom presupposes that the basic belief pattern of the population is that of the Christian faith and that Christian ethical standards are the norm. This model can remain viable despite a fair amount of dissent from individuals, but there comes a time when the whole community moves into a post-Christendom situation and Christendom is replaced by the 'secular' model. This is the position in much of Europe at present, but it is much complicated by the rapid changes which are taking place in the secular model. For instance, Robin Gill has rightly called into question the common presupposition that the alternative to Christianity is secularism. It is too soon to be sure what is emerging, but rather than the cool rationalism of atheism it seems that the likelihood is a smorgasbord of beliefs – ranging from the most debased of superstitions, through a belief in scientism, to faiths which are based entirely on experience. Post-modernism is not fertile ground for atheism.

The division between the two tectonic plates is becoming much more obvious. Christian faith and Christian ethics are no longer seen as being virtually coterminous with the faith and ethics of society at large. Christian values are not enshrined in legislation (as began to happen so soon after the coming of St Augustine to Kent), and popular attitudes no longer reflect some sort of Christian background. The ritualistic remnants like the coronation and the place of the bishops in the House of Lords look increasingly dated. The Church becomes both more marginalised and more distinct from its surroundings. This is bewildering for many, but may give the Church a sharper edge and more self-confidence when the divergence becomes more obvious.

The corollary of this is that conflict between the Church and secular society becomes much more likely – indeed can already be seen over a variety of subjects ranging from matters to do with the family to the effect of economic policy on the poor and attitudes to the hugely popular National Lottery. On the Continent one response has been the establishment of political parties, usually called Christian Democrats, which seek to maintain a close link between the thinking and practice of the Church and of secular society. This is not an option that has ever had much chance of success in the UK, and seems to be declining in several other countries. In the United States various fundamentalist groups have formed the 'Christian Coalition' which seeks to take over an existing political party. But the chances of either option being able to maintain a 'Christendom' solution seem remote. In the name of tolerance all things become possible, and the Church becomes no more than yet another pressure group.

The same process can be seen in Islam. It too is a mega-culture – a tectonic plate which looks for a total commitment of faith. It too has its equivalent of 'Christendom', though much more nearly intact, in the Islamic countries. It too is colliding with the other plate of secular mega-culture and many are the volcanoes which spurt at the boundary and the earthquakes which shake the ground.

In the evangelisation of England we can see what happened when a new faith leapt into a pagan land, when two mega-cultures collided. We can also see the formation of a Christendom which endured for 1,400 years.

The formation of Christendom

In the British Museum there is the Franks Casket, so called because it was bought in Paris by Sir A. W. Franks in 1867, after being used as a sewing box in a French farmhouse. It is made of walrus ivory and various scenes are carved on the sides and lid. One of the scenes is thoroughly biblical – the presentation of gifts to the infant Jesus by the wise men. But one other panel shows gruesome Anglo-Saxon myths about Wayland the Smith and the Swan maidens. Another scene about Romulus and Remus comes from Roman mythology. Another shows a historical event, the capture of Jerusalem by Titus. One single object made shortly after the evangelisation of England shows the merging of different belief systems. In other words, Christianity did not destroy the old faith: it supplanted it over a period of centuries. The very fact that we have retained the old names for the days of the week despite their origin as the names of pagan gods is an indication of this assimilation: Tuesday from Tiu; Wednesday from Woden; Thursday from Thor; Friday from Frei.

One possibility when faith systems collide is for the one to destroy the other – as seems to have happened earlier when the Anglo-Saxons invaded England and destroyed Christianity along with the population. This was also taking place at much the same time in North Africa, as Islam swept along the coastal area and destroyed the ancient churches where St Augustine of Hippo had ministered, and moving northward across the Straits of Gibraltar captured almost all of Spain in 711, turning churches into mosques and altering the religion of a whole people.

The other alternative when two faith systems collide is for a 'conversion' process to take place. The Anglo-Saxons, having destroyed the original Christianity of England, were in their turn converted by it. As we shall see there was the power of the gospel which led to this, but we should not be blind to social factors operating at the same time.

Anglo-Saxon belief

An understanding of the mega-culture of the Anglo-Saxons helps us to understand their reaction to the Christian faith, what elements the Christian evangelists were able to use to forward the gospel, and why it was ultimately successful. Their belief patterns can chiefly be gauged by evidence from the Low Countries where they originated, and, with caution, from Scandinavia.

There is a danger in assuming that all the invaders had a similar religious structure, for they were members of different tribes. However there seem to have been common factors. Paganism is only in part to do with the worship of the gods: it seeks to explain the inexplicable phenomena such as thunder and natural growth; it gives a framework to social life through rituals for marriage and childbearing. Above all it tries to come to terms with illness and death.

Paganism does not demand intellectual coherence. The Anglo-Saxon pantheon is difficult to disentangle, for the gods are known to us through a series of stories, and they play different parts in each. Thus there is evidence that Woden took over the role of chief god from Thor, and the goddess of fertility goes through many names and guises. Moreover mythologies blend and borrow: for example Baldur the Brave has links with the far off Babylonian Tammuz.[3]

It is therefore difficult to decide what the exact mythology of the Anglo-Saxons was. For our purposes what is important is the way in which the Christian faith used elements from pagan mythology for evangelistic purposes, and either assimilated or destroyed the religious infrastructure of priests and temples.

As might be expected, charms and incantations persisted for long after the period of evangelisation. Sometimes they merely change their personnel. One charm for a sprained ankle merely replaced Baldur and Woden with Father, Son and Holy Spirit. Long into the Christian era Wednesday was thought to be a good day for sowing the corn, though few farmers linked it with the power of Woden who was thought to bring good luck.

Christian missionaries have always found it difficult to evangelise a polytheistic society, for often Christ is merely accepted as a
new god to be put alongside the others. Famously King Raedwald
of the East Angles suggested that a figure of Christ be placed in
the temple with the other gods so that he could be a Christian but
also worship the gods of his ancestors. Even today Christian
workers in polytheistic lands find it easy to get people to acknowledge Christ but hard to get that profession to make any difference.

We have to recognise that for many peasants and ordinary
Anglo-Saxons conversion meant mainly the supplanting of one lot
of stories by another. Instead of the familiar stories of Valhalla
and the tricks of Loki, there were stories of a birth in a stable and
someone who fed crowds and healed lepers. Deeper than that were
more archetypal images of death and rebirth in the stories about
the crucifixion and empty tomb which took the place of the stories
in Anglo-Saxon mythology where Baldur was the 'bleeding god'
and Thor brought his goats back to life. In both sets of stories
evil is snake-shaped – as the subtle beast in the garden of Eden
and as the great World Serpent which encircled the earth. But
more significant than the details of the myths is the mind-set
which they imply.

Wyrd

Central to the Anglo-Saxon attitude was *wyrd*. Its root meaning
is 'fate' or 'destiny'. A secondary meaning is 'a fateful event' –
what happened when wyrd overtook you. Wyrd was irresistible,
unbending and certain: if such was one's wyrd then there was no
gainsaying it. It had to be accepted with as much stoical acceptance
as one could muster.

When the Christian gospel arrived it introduced another irresistible object, Almighty God. For a time these two – wyrd and God
– held uneasy sway together in people's minds. There was an initial
confusion, for Christ as a man was seen as being subject to wyrd
as all human beings are. Hence one of the 'Gnomic Poems' says
'The glories of Christ are great; Wyrd is strongest of all'. In its
secondary meaning as the time when one's wyrd was enacted, the
crucifixion was seen as the time when Christ encountered his
destiny. In *The Dream of the Rood* the poet dreams of the very
cross on which Christ was crucified, now surrounded by light and

bedecked with jewels. Despite the adornments, the dreamer could still perceive the marks of crucifixion and the blood of Christ. And then the Rood speaks, describing the journey it had made since the time it was cut down in the forest until it was set on a hill when 'the young hero' mounted it. The Rood says, 'I have endured many terrible wyrds upon the hill.'[4]

This belief that fate governed life was widespread and led to a second attitude. Your wyrd was to be fortunate or the opposite. Luck was something which you either had or did not have: you were lucky or unlucky, and there was nothing you could do about it. Sometimes your luck ran out and you became unlucky: at Stamford Bridge in 1066 Harold of England remarked grimly of Harold Sigurdson who was losing the battle, 'a great man of stately appearance, but I think his luck has left him'. It is sometimes used as if it is equivalent to 'mana' or 'aura' (in a semi-spiritualistic sense).

Sacrifice

A third element was that of sacrifice. Offerings had to be made. Sometimes these would be of crops or livestock but a darker note enters, for human sacrifice was not unknown. Prisoners seem to have been frequently offered to the gods and Bede refers to 30 or more people leaping off a cliff as a sacrifice to Woden at a time of famine. Archaeologists have found skeletons of people who seem to have been buried alive; others have been decapitated or garotted.[5]

Feasting

Central to belief was the companionship of the feast. This needs more explanation. Anglo-Saxon literature is saturated by the atmosphere of the great hall where the eating and carousing took place. The halls were of considerable size as the excavations at Old Yeavering in Northumberland bear witness. They must have been thronged for most of the day for men and women worked there, ate there, slept there and relaxed there. And a principal relaxation was the feast, which was 'the pleasure of the rich and the solace of the poor'.[6]

As we shall see in the next chapter a king tempted warriors to his standard and kept their loyalty by offering gifts and a good time. For Anglo-Saxons a good time seems to have meant being provided with ample food and much drink in the presence of their king.

Along with the feast there had to be entertainment. This seems to have taken two forms. The more refined was that provided by the skald who sang long sagas. Some of these were intended to flatter the king with interminable genealogies showing how his line went back to famous, even divine ancestors. Alternatively they were exciting tales of battle and adventure and love. Although the people were illiterate there was a long tradition of oral poetry and song.[7] Later on it came to be written down, and the restless spirit of *The Seafarer* and the plight of *The Wanderer* are not merely among the earliest but also some of the finest examples of English poetry. It is not surprising that in this setting the idea of the hall became central to belief. *Beowulf* has most of its action in and around the hall, and Valhalla was seen as a larger and longer party for the warriors as they whiled away the time before the final battle against the giants of evil.

Less refined entertainment came when drink had taken its toll and boisterous games of physical prowess followed: those used to modern service life will recognise the pattern immediately. However, they enjoyed crueller sports than is common on Mess Night. One was to shoot apples or gaming pieces from the head of unpopular or weak people with their arrows, William Tell style; and as alcohol unsteadied their aim, death was not uncommon. Another 'sport' was to put a victim in a corner and throw at him the bones which were left after the feasting. Since Christians would not have been the most popular roisterers they must have found themselves in the corner often enough and a shower of ox bones cannot have been pleasant. Two saints, Edmund and Alphege, are said to have been martyred in this way.[8]

Pagan priesthood

The story of the conversion of Edwin illustrates the practice of pagan religion. The long discussion between Edwin and his nobles about whether or not the king should be baptised was dramatically ended when the high priest Coifi leapt onto a horse. He rode to his own temple and defiled it by throwing a spear into it. He deliberately broke two taboos, 'for it is not permitted for a priest of the sacrifices to bear arms or ride a stallion'.

We can see here that Anglo-Saxon religion had a professional priesthood who offered sacrifices in a temple. From elsewhere we know that the temples were usually built of wood, often on the brow of a hill. Certain clearings in the great forests which surrounded every Anglo-Saxon community were also held as sacred. Allied to this there was a veneration of wooden pillars, which may have had overtones of the great Yggdrasil, the earth tree on which all depended, and of which our maypoles may be feeble descendants. Pillars of wood set up as door posts had particular significance and by Viking times these were endowed with magic properties: the first settlers approaching Iceland brought their door-pillars with them, and when nearing land threw them overboard. Where they were washed ashore the settlers built their new homes.[9]

The priests also practised a secret art known only to them – writing. In an emergent society this is often seen as sacred. Because it is understood by few, it is mysterious and magical. The Celtic priests used the script called ogam and Anglo-Saxons used runic writing. It was a mystical craft reserved to them, and no doubt they emphasised the wondrous nature of their skill.

Why did the Christian faith succeed?

When we ask the question 'Why did the Christian faith supplant the old?' there are various answers. It has been suggested[10] that the old religion of myth and battle did not suit the more settled social conditions which they now encountered and that the Christian faith seemed more sophisticated and urbane. The new faith was mature and well thought through by obviously intelligent and enthusiastic people. It faced the problem of illness and death not with charms and luck but with faith and hope. There was a framework of heaven and hell which gave purpose to human existence. There were patterns of behaviour for individuals which made sense and made the old ways seem uncouth and savage. It was a religion of writing, not hidden away in mystic runes but open to all who were prepared to be educated.

There was another element. All religions are ultimately doomed unless they can be seen to change things. The new faith came to the Anglo-Saxons with miracle and wonder. All the Christian writings from this era are heavy with tales of the power of God at work; indeed they embarrass our modern minds, brought up on Enlightenment presuppositions that such things do not take place. Many of these stories bring to mind the battle between Moses and the magicians of Pharaoh: after each of the first three plagues, 'the Egyptian magicians did the same thing by their spells' – but they failed on the maggots, and had to declare 'It is the hand of God'.[11] The pagan priests and the Christian missionary tried to outdo each other in miracle, because the people thought that it showed that God was on the side of the strongest.

Above all Christianity was a religion which claimed to be a religion of truth, passionately advocated by men and women who seemed more concerned about communicating their message than about their own personal safety or welfare.

Today

Does our evangelism and ministry to people take seriously enough the cultures – mega-, midi- and mini – which people inhabit? In particular, is the Church looking closely enough at the conflict between the 'tectonic plates' which is taking place with the demise of Christendom, and is it preparing for the increasingly violent clashes which will take place on the boundary?

Present-day belief patterns suggest that many are turning to pre-Christian Anglo-Saxon ways of thinking – belief in an inexorable Fate and in luck (seen at its most obvious in the razzmatazz surrounding the National Lottery). This breeds fatalism and a 'nothing-you-can-do-about-it' attitude.

Some are going further and seeing the need to propitiate this Fate with sacrifice. Superstitions are returning to haunt the recesses of people's minds.

Conversion did not entirely banish the old faith, and in the 890s Pope Formosus wrote to England to warn that 'the nefarious rites of the pagans have sprouted again in your parts', and condemned 'incantations and auguries, the veneration of stones, trees and wells, magic potions, ancient customs concerning the sun and moon, and witchcraft'.

Deep in the papers of the Vatican is a catechism St Boniface used for Saxons who found Christ in his ministry in Germany:

> V: Do you forsake the devil?
> R: I do forsake the devil.
> V: And all the devil's bribes?
> R: And I forsake all the devil's bribes.
> V: And all the devil's works?
> R: And I forsake all the devil's works and words,
>   Thunor and Woden and Saxnote
>   and all the unclean spirits who are their friends.

These early Christians knew the power of evil and sought to root it out of people's thinking. The growth of modern superstition and the re-invasion of the human psyche with concepts of luck have once again to be addressed by the Church. Much is obvious and public like the 'what the Stars say' columns in glossy magazines and the TV astrologers. Less obvious and more dangerous are the groups meddling with ouija boards, consulting clairvoyants and allowing their lives to be ruled by horoscopes. I knew one woman who had consulted a clairvoyant and been told 'You will never be happy as long as you live in that house.' She immediately went out and ordered in the bulldozers, building a new house on the ruins of the old.

Once again Christians need the 'circle' prayer of protection. The Celts discovered 'spiritual warfare' long ago, as can be seen in 'St Patrick's Breastplate', possibly from the eighth century.

> Against all Satan's spells and wiles,
> Against false words of heresy,
> Against the knowledge that defiles,
> Against the heart's idolatry,
> Against the wizard's evil craft,
> Against the death-wound and the burning,
> The choking wave, the poisoned shaft,
> Protect me Christ, till thy returning.

Notes

1 According to INFORM, June 1995.
2 It has also to be said that modern cosmology is being forced to rethink its Enlightenment presupposition about the random meaninglessness of the universe. So many factors have to be so finely balanced – the strength of the force of gravity, the electric charge and mass of an

electron etc. – that the chance creation of the sort of universe which could have produced the life apparent on this planet is so improbable as to be ridiculous. Some have even begun to posit a Mind behind it all. It is like drinking coffee – some prefer their Anthropic Principle weak, others like it strong.

3 Tammuz is mentioned in Ezekiel 8.14.

4 Scholars believe that, although the poem in its final form is probably eleventh-century, it contains earlier elements – extraordinarily a quotation from it is carved in runes on a Saxon cross preserved at Ruthwell in Dumfries which is certainly centuries earlier. It is a sophisticated and moving poem.

5 Inevitably there is discussion as to whether these are ritual offerings or examples of capital punishment. It is impossible to be certain.

6 R. I. Page, *Life in Anglo-Saxon England* (1970).

7 In the first century Tacitus had described the 'ancient songs' of the Germanic tribes as their only way of remembering or recording the past.

8 For an account of what this part of an Anglo-Saxon feast was like, see Ian Macdougall, 'Serious entertainments: a peculiar type of Viking atrocity' in *Anglo-Saxon England* 22 (1993).

9 This reverence for wooden columns existed in Christian times, for the pillar against which St Aidan died was long venerated: indeed it may still be extant as one of the roof timbers of Bamburgh Church.

10 Among others by H. R. Lyon, *Anglo-Saxon England and the Norman Conquest* (1991).

11 Exodus 7.22 and 8.18f.

Chapter 7

The King

TO THIS day the Coronation Service has Anglo-Saxon overtones. The people affirm the choice of the new monarch and he or she is also invested with an almost priestly character. They are seen as not only the people's choice but also as chosen by God. The Stuarts' tenacious belief in the divine right of kings was a major factor in bringing about the English Civil War, for they argued that they were above the law of the land and answerable only to the God who had chosen them. Even today it is not possible directly to sue the Crown. Wisps of the old doctrine still lurk in constitutional corners.

In thinking about the evangelism of England it is impossible to ignore the place of the king. We have already seen how crucial the conversion of the king was in leading to the conversion of his kingdom, and how a reversion to paganism often followed the accession of a pagan king.

When the Anglo-Saxons were in the Low Countries the 'kings' were little more than tribal chiefs. They were chosen by the people for their prowess rather than their family. Wisdom and skill in battle seem to have been the main requirements for success in the election, together with that essential Anglo-Saxon ingredient – luck. This was the mana which showed that the gods smiled on him, and the people, in making their choice, merely recognised that fact. As an ancient proverb had it, 'It is hard to fight against a king's luck'.

Once chosen the king-elect was acclaimed on the howe, the tribal centre. No doubt there would have been elaborate rites and sacrifices; there would certainly have been feasting and rejoicing.

After this the king became the focus of the tribe. It was important as soon as possible to establish his legitimacy as someone of good blood: this was done by rewriting his lineage so that he was seen to be descended from many famous people. But mortal ancestry was not enough. He had also to be shown to have divine origins, and so his family tree was traced back after many generations to the gods, so that he could describe himself as 'Woden-sprung'. Part of the job of the skald was to make sure that everyone was aware of the fact, and genealogies grew to more than biblical proportions. Since the king was descended from the gods he was now himself semi-divine and, as such, was expected to bring fertility to the crops, good fortune in battle and booty in plenty. As someone who was the tribal point of contact with the gods the king performed a priestly role, making sacrifices to ensure victory and prosperity, for he was 'the personal embodiment of the link with the divine on which the tribe's well-being depends'.[1] Allied to this was an expectation that the king could heal. Waldemar I of Denmark touched the seed that it might grow well and the children that they might prosper. While 'touching for the King's evil' (scrofula) was probably started no earlier than the eleventh century, kings had long been regarded as having healing powers.

Riches were the proof of the king's 'luck', flowing as they did from the fertility of the land and success in war. They were an essential element in the socio-political life of the tribe, for warriors were the people who won wars and they had to be attracted by the promise of booty. This came from successful campaigns against other tribes; we know how troublesome the Saxon 'pirates' were to late Roman Britain as they harried the coastal areas, carrying off spoils and slaves. 'Gift-giving' became a necessary part of a king's life and the old poems are full of praise for the king who was generous. It must not be assumed that the warriors were nothing more than mercenaries, for while the king gave them riches (often the gold rings beloved by the poets) so they in return gave him loyalty. Treachery to the lord you had sworn to follow to the end was the ultimate disgrace and to flee from the battle while the king was still present and alive branded you a coward to the end of your days.

If it was clear that his god-given 'luck' had deserted him the king could be deposed or even killed. Olaf of Tretelgia was accused of failing to make the sacrifices and since this was supposed to have made the crops fail, he was burned in his house as a sacrifice to Woden.

In later generations it would be recognised that the need to ensure a constant stream of booty led to an unstable society, particularly after the small tribes of Germany became considerable kingdoms in England. If a nation had to be continually at war in order to assure a steady supply of plunder then it was impossible to fulfil the other expectation of the king – that he was to be the *rex pacificus*, the 'peace-king' who enforced the laws and gave stability and peace in his realms.

A further consequence of the king's semi-divine status was that as the link with the gods he was a sort of high priest to whom the other priests, despite their skills, were subject. Because of this, if he wished to ally the tribe with another god he was free to do so, though, as Edwin's story shows, this could have considerable political implications. Since he was the central religious focus, if he thought that he and the tribe should follow a god whom he thought to be stronger or better, others would follow obediently. The importance of this for the evangelisation of an area is obvious, and it explains why the early missionaries made straight for royalty.

Once the king was converted, benefits for the new religion followed quickly because the power of the state would be thrown behind the new faith. After his conversion Eaconberht of Kent (640–664) passed laws to enforce the keeping of Lent and the destruction of idols. A little later Ine of Wessex in his codification of the law required that children should be baptised, and forbade working on Sunday. At the king's elbow sat his advisers, who now included church leaders; it is not surprising that the codifications, which copied the Roman model, should have such a strongly Christian content.

Successful invasions make minor figures into major ones. Just as the Norman invasion led to the country squires of Normandy becoming mighty barons in England, the Anglo-Saxon invasion made tribal kings into rulers of considerable domains. But the aura that surrounded the head of the tribal king survived the passage across the North Sea and was indeed enhanced by his greater power. Conversion to Christianity did not diminish it. The need

to have 'sound' ancestors still remained and converted rulers sometimes tried to conflate the pagan and the Christian with comic
results. One king claimed he was descended from 'Woden, who is
the son of Sceaf, who is the son of Noah and was born in Noah's
ark'.

After kings were converted the Church played much the same
role as the former pagan priesthood – offering sacrifices and advice.
The Church was always wary of the power of sacral kingship,
possibly seeing it as a threat to episcopal power: few churches
were dedicated to saint-kings. However the link between state and
Church played a major part in the advancement of the gospel
and the relationship between the king and the bishop came to play
a vital part in the smooth running of society. The king and the
bishop needed each other – the king needed the Church to affirm
his authority and provide a unifying element in his kingdom, and
the Church needed the king to advance the gospel. In the early
days we see kings actively involved in preaching and travelling
with the early missionaries.

The first Christian consecration of a king seems to have been
that of Ecgfrith in 787. The link was complete: church leaders
recognised that this man was chosen by God as their sovereign
and the bishops pledged their loyalty to him. It can be taken as a
convenient date to mark the beginnings of Christendom, for the
tectonic plates were becoming coterminous. The Christian faith
and contemporary society now had the same boundaries.

The place of the bishops

The early bishops were monks, and often of humble birth. But it
is noticeable how soon many church leaders began to come from
the aristocracy, like Wilfred and many of the abbots and abbesses.
The link with the monastery disappeared and bishops become
politicians and courtiers as well as churchmen. This was accentu-
ated by the previous practice of the Saxon tribes of having advisers
close to the king.[2] In pagan times the priests often fulfilled this
role – they were guardians of the tribe's secrets and history and
were probably intelligent and wily. Inevitably the bishops and
senior clergy came to play the same role: they were literate, clever
and often worldly wise. Long after the Anglo-Saxon period

churchmen played a major role as agents of government. Only in the last two centuries has the role of senior churchmen in running the country diminished, for it was part of the way in which Christendom flourished where Church and state worked closely together, theoretically for the good of the whole people. Many of the state prayers in the Book of Common Prayer breathe this atmosphere and to this day Anglican bishops sit in the House of Lords.

If the Church was now important to the state, then the doings of the Church demanded royal attention. It was the King, Oswiu of Northumbria, who summoned the great Synod of Whitby in 664 because of the difficulties produced in his kingdom by the differences between Roman and Celtic practices. Indeed in his own household different dates for celebrating Easter were causing domestic chaos. It was he who sat in judgement and played an active part in the proceedings.

Since bishops were now important people within the state, kings were not content for them to be chosen only by the Church. If these men were to be their closest advisers they expected to have a hand in their appointment. And kings were not looking for holy men in monasteries but for people who could handle matters of state with wise gravity. The Pope kept his hand on appointments, but for many centuries there were frequent tussles between European monarchs and Rome about appointments to bishoprics. In countries where the Reformation occurred the Pope was ignored and even more power was put in the hands of the secular authorities. To this day Anglican bishops are chosen ultimately by the Queen on the advice of her ministers – though the present concordat means that the church is the prime mover in putting names forward.

The *comitatus*

In the first century Tacitus described the Germanic tribes as 'wild, blue-eyed, reddish-haired and large-framed . . . courageous fighters, but impatient of hard work'. They seem to have been easily bored and used to wander off in search of adventure. The *comitatus* or war-band was the theme of much Anglo-Saxon literature – and was idealised in the stories of the knights of Arthur and the

Round Table. It was an extreme example of male-bonding with the emphasis on mutual support, courage and loyalty. The warriors spent their life in the king's hall in constant fighting, boasting and horseplay. As Tacitus said of their forefathers, 'No nation abandons itself more completely to banqueting than the German . . . drinking bouts lasting a day and a night are considered in no way disgraceful.' However, they were not just a lot of lager louts: they owed fealty to their lord and would fight courageously to protect him. Two of the finest early poems speak of the lostness of someone who is 'alone, without any company', who has lost his lord and the companionship of his fellow warriors.[3]

The king needed to keep his *comitatus* happy and at his disposal. Gold and plenty of mead were the traditional way to ensure this. They also needed plenty of excitement: after all, their *raison d'être* was to fight. As a result a king was not supposed to take his Christian faith too seriously: Sigebert of the East Saxons was murdered by bored companions 'because he was too apt to spare his enemies and forgive the wrongs they had done him'.

The warrior band around the king came to have less importance as the Germanic tribes moved into England. Domains were larger and kings did not always lead their armies out to war personally: there was less need for such a band of committed warriors and kings had more need for leaders of armies and makers of policy than for fighters. Sometimes the *comitatus* was changed into a personal bodyguard, at other times it withered away.

Nevertheless it is not difficult to see the ease with which the Anglo-Saxons drew links between the *comitatus* and the apostles: the band around the leader was part of their thinking and often they use the language of the *comitatus* to describe Christian discipleship. Thus the early poem *Christ* describes a biblical incident in language which would have been meaningful to the poet's audience:

> The mighty Lord, the Prince of Splendour, who summoned his
> thegns,
> the well-loved band, to Bethany.

The apostles were described as *cohors militum Christi* – a platoon of Christian soldiers.

The lure of Rome

The Germanic tribes had long had contact with the Roman Empire. In the beginning they fought them, and inflicted several heavy defeats on the legions. Later they traded. Significantly, in the language they brought over to England there were over 100 words with Latin origins – mainly to do with war or trade. Population figures must be approximate but the best guess is that there were two or three million of them, compared with 20 to 30 million in the Roman Empire.

From their limited knowledge of Rome the barbarians had come to wonder at and admire the Empire, even though they themselves had contributed to its decline. From these tribes had come the Angles, the Saxons and the Jutes.

When they came to England they must have marvelled at the roads and the ruined buildings left behind when the Romans departed. Even in decay the forums and the villas and the amphitheatres and the baths must have seemed supernatural in their size and scope. A poet looking awestruck at the ruins of Bath wrote:

> Well-wrought this wall: Wyrd broke it.
> The stronghold burst . . .
> And the wielders and the wrights?
> Earthgrip holds them – gone, long gone,
> fast in graves grasp while fifty fathers and sons have passed.
>
> Bright were the buildings, halls where springs ran,
> high, horngabled, much throng noise;
> these many meadhalls men filled
> with loud cheerfulness: Wyrd changed that.
>
> Stood stone houses: wide streams welled
> hot from source . . .[4]

They were impressed, and their kings and court began to see Roman civilisation as something to be desired for themselves and not just as a convenient pile of potential plunder. Their previous way of life began to seem uncivilised and unsophisticated, and, being socially upwardly mobile, they began to want what they encountered. When the great hoard at Sutton Hoo was dug up, it opened for us a window into the life of a powerful Anglo-Saxon soon after the invasions. It is probably the burial of Raedwald of East Anglia in 616. The old tribal way of doing things is still there

– he is buried in a ship. But his treasures and possessions betoken something new, for they were far more sumptuous than his predecessors could ever have dreamed of. Some of it has Roman origins. There is a magnificent Byzantine silver plate; the helmet is German, but is a copy of a Roman original, the gold coins came from Gaul. There are Christian emblems on a couple of spoons – though whether this represents the faith of Raedwald or is merely booty is hard to say.

The changeover to Roman ways was surprisingly rapid in some areas of life. In particular the use of writing for mundane as well as magical purposes meant many changes. The king Ethelbert of Kent who met Augustine when he landed was the first king in England to write down and codify his laws; it would be interesting to know how far Augustine, the former administrator of a monastery near Rome, had a hand in suggesting this. Kings began to issue written titles to property and to evolve a primitive bureaucracy. Richard Hodges says of the new gentry: 'They wanted to become Roman noblemen, not Roman peasants . . . they took over the political system, the social hierarchy, the Christian religion and the local industries of the Roman Empire with little alteration.'[5] Slowly coinage was reintroduced and trade was able to rise above mere barter.

The idea of a resurrection of the Roman Empire must have been in people's minds for a long time. For an Anglo-Saxon king or bishop the time of the Empire must have seemed a period of unparalleled peace and social harmony. As we have seen, Gregory had the idea of a new Christianised Empire. In the East, Constantinople saw itself as 'the new Rome' and the Emperor as successor to the Caesars. A little later Charlemagne had inscribed on his seal, 'The Renewal of the Roman Empire'. The dream of the Holy Roman Empire lasted for a millennium and until 1917 Russian Emperors saw themselves as Caesars (Tsars) over Holy Russia which was, for them, the third incarnation of the Empire. It was they who had inherited the mantle of a heretical Rome and a Byzantium that had fallen to the infidels.

The clergy (especially those from a Roman background) were examples of a more educated, more urban way of life. Even in Ireland as early as the sixth century priests were told to conform with 'civilised' Roman ways by wearing a tunic, shaving their head and seeing that their wives were veiled.

How far was the conversion of England merely one aspect of this Romanisation? It certainly did not seem like that at the time as Christianity came and, after first prospering, was thrown back on the defensive in the 630s. With hindsight it would have been remarkable if peoples who were surrounded by Christian countries could have kept to the old ways for long but one does not need to do more than read what was written at the time, imagine the unremitting prayers and devotion of the early saints and see what their heritage has been to realise that this was not mere conformity to a social convention but something which in the hearts of many people went deep into the spiritual realm. No doubt the kings were being pressurised to convert by the 650s and 660s when it became the fashionable thing to do but for many it was more than an action of statecraft. As early as the 630s King Sigebert of the East Angles abdicated in favour of another member of his family and entered a monastery. When Penda invaded East Anglia Sigebert's people dragged him out of the monastery to give heart to the troops, but he refused to go into battle with anything more than a stick – sadly it did him little good: the East Angles were defeated and Sigebert killed. At one point so many members of royal families were entering monasteries that some were asking who were going to rule the land. These are not the actions of people to whom faith is no more than a political action.

Kingship and deity

Not surprisingly we find that their experience of kingship is transferred to God in the thought and worship of the Anglo-Saxons. There is much use of such phrases as 'King of kings and Lord of lords' which must have been more meaningful in days when England had a dozen kings and many lords. For the peasant crushed by the exactions of the aristocracy, it must have brought a little comfort to know that his lord had someone above him to whom he would have to give account. The Anglo-Saxon word 'Frey' which means 'Lord' became a common name for Christ.

Heaven becomes 'the Hall of Christ', a Christian version of Valhalla. For many their mental picture must have been of the king's hall, only in this case it was the Lord of lords giving gifts from his high seat to those who are his companions. To be invited to feast with the king was honour indeed, to be invited by the King of kings was magnificence. Alternatively heaven was described as a 'fair and fertile plain where fruits are to be had for the picking'.[6] For a peasant the thought of harvest without work would indeed have been heaven.

Hell was something different – a place of torment. In a world where torture was almost as common as it is today and when illness had no respite except death, the idea of eternal pain was not difficult to envisage and to shudder at. Bede was not afraid to 'dangle people over the pit' as his tales about unrepentant sinners show, for they were designed to be didactic stories to frighten people into repentance: thus his account of the drunken smith led 'many people to do penance for their sins without delay. And may the reading of this account have the same effect.'[7]

Social changes

The coming of the new faith meant a change in morality and social outlook. When they were in the Low Countries each tribe had a social order in which everyone knew their place, but the smallness of the communities meant that there would have been a good deal of sympathy with each other's position. When the larger kingdoms were established in England society became more stratified. At the bottom of the heap were the slaves. The Church spoke against slavery in a rather half-hearted sort of way for it was seen as being contrary to the Faith – slowly it disappeared, though in England it lasted longer than in most places in Europe.

The Christian gospel could never have been seen to square with the Anglo-Saxon love of violence, and once the immediate turmoil of the invasions was over and the main kingdoms established, warfare and the need for warriors diminished. Disputes were settled by treaty and royal marriages rather than carnage. The bishops at the king's right hand may have been worldly but they were still bishops and counselled moderation and peace. On the whole the eighth century was a time of peace, until the first Vikings came in its final years to presage a more violent ninth century.

In pagan times wives were property: they could be bought and sold and divorce was easy. The Church sought to prevent the misuse of women in this way and to make divorce harder – though it was not prohibited: Archbishop Theodore tried to restrict it to those who had been deserted for five years or had been carried-off to slavery from which there was no reasonable chance of escape. There were also constant condemnations of incest by the Church – but as the prohibited degrees were so wide and village communities so small it was difficult for people to find partners who were not 'family'.

Today

In Anglo-Saxon times evangelism was simpler. First you identified the king and then you brought the gospel to him. Since they were regarded as semi-divine, their people assumed that they were trustworthy guides in religious matters and followed them. The early missionaries knew that once the kings and the court were converted they would lead their peoples to Christ.

We have to be careful in reading the old stories not to be misled by the emphasis on royalty. At a glance it might be assumed that the first missionaries did nothing but encounter kings, get them converted and then let the state do the rest. We need to remember the thousands of unsung heroes – those monks and nuns, lay and ordained, who went from village to village preaching and teaching despite constant harassment from the followers of the old faith and considerable physical danger. We get glimpses of their activity when we hear of Paulinus baptising thousands and unnamed priests healing the sick. There are also stories about encounters between village peasants and the missionaries – and relationships were not always smooth, as in Bede's tale of the monks who had lost their oars and were drifting out to sea – while the villagers jeered at them from the bank.

But the emphasis of the stories is right. The encounters between the Church and the royal households were not merely more exciting literature but also more significant historically and spiritually. The conversion of a king led to the conversion of a people. Even the Pope in Rome knew this, for Gregory and to a lesser extent his successors sent a stream of letters to the contemporary kings urging them to come to faith or, after their conversion, giving advice on the matters which concerned a Christian monarch.

Who are the 'kings' of today? Anglo-Saxon kings were nothing if not opinion-formers – as they thought, so did others. If the Christian faith seemed attractive and worthwhile to the king then his kingdom would eventually become Christian. Where he led many followed.

In the days of Christendom, and to some extent even today, the Church is able to make its voice heard. But there is a difference. Previously it had access to the heart of the nation, now it is little more than a pressure group shouting from the outskirts of the crowd: important, but no more so than a dozen other groups. In the media, in political life, in consideration of moral issues, its power has shrunk. One only has to look the part which the Church of England played in the Abdication Crisis of 1936, compared with its present influence over royal matrimonial affairs, to realise that the impact which it or any other denomination can have today is severely limited.

As Dean Acheson said of Britain, the Church 'has lost an empire and not yet found a role'. It tries to retain as many of its remaining links with the political, civic and commercial life of the nation as possible. But it is a power which is still draining away. At the same time it has not yet learned how to be an effective pressure group – manipulating the media, simplifying the issues, bellowing so that it can be heard above the clatter of the marketplace. It is not the way things have been done in the past, where the quiet word and climbing the backstairs have been more usual. But if the other avenues are shut against us we have to make a noise, distasteful though it may be to many.

It was not distasteful to our Lord. To make people hear he made very public protests, as in the Temple; he preached to the crowds outside the safety of a religious building; he received important people late at night; he stirred up strife; he exaggerated to make his point; he engaged in public argument. Quite literally he 'made an exhibition of himself', and finally 'he exposed himself to death',[8] the final public demonstration.

It is said of Greenpeace that they take five minutes to make a decision and an hour deciding how it is to be presented to the world. The Church, on the other hand, spends hours making decisions and barely a minute in deciding on public presentation. As a result the impact of the Christian gospel through the Church is diminishing. The former quiet ways no longer have an effect and we have not learnt the brashness which is needed to hold our own in the television studio, through the planted piece in the newspapers or through public demonstrations.

The only Christians who have learned this lesson are those who tend to be one-issue enthusiasts (for or against) on such subjects as abortion, homosexuality or women priests. Their demonstrations, letters to the papers and the public profile of some of their protagonists are picked up by the media and their stance is well known. Unfortunately the issues they choose tend to give the impression that the Church is only concerned about sex and gender. The majesty of the Christian gospel and the wholesomeness of Christian moral standards go by default because ordinary non-churchgoers (and a surprising number of those who do go to church) do not know what 'the Church stands for'.

The dangers of such a public stance are obvious – oversimplification of serious issues, conflict, personality cult. But it is better to get over a simple message than no message, better to risk conflict than to 'die with dignity', better to allow a person to be identified with a position if that is necessary to get the message heard. Like the early missionaries the Church must go to the places of power and accept, as they did, the inevitable compromises and criticisms.

Notes

1 William A. Chaney, *The Cult of Kingship in Anglo-Saxon England* (1970); the whole subject of sacral kingship is one of considerable debate and complexity.

2 The same need for advisers can be seen in many parts of the Bible: e.g. 2 Samuel 17.23 where Ahithophel hangs himself because his advice was disregarded.

3 *The Wanderer* and *The Seafarer* – both go beyond the lone traveller to discuss metaphysical questions about the meaning of life itself.

4 *The Ruin*, translated by Michael Alexander in *The Earliest English Poems* (1966).

5 *The Making of Britain: The Dark Ages* (1984).

6 H. R. Lyon, *Anglo-Saxon England and the Norman Conquest* (1991).

7 Bede, *Ecclesiastical History* 5.14.

8 Isaiah 53.12.

Chapter 8

Celt versus Roman

TOO MANY history books which tell the story of the Synod of Whitby regard it as a dispute about trifles. They usually cite the differences in the dating of Easter and the shape of the monastic tonsure with the suggestion that these are not matters which adults should get steamed up about, and is just the church making much out of nothing as usual. However the issues were far more numerous and far more important and had a long history behind them.

Roman and British bishops

When Augustine was sent by Gregory the possibility of conflict with the bishops who were already in Britain was obvious. British bishops were still in Wales, the South West and, probably, the North West, and were still ministering to the refugee British and the Welsh.

Bede did not think much of the British. In a famous passage he recorded his view of the British Christians before Augustine's arrival:

> Among other unspeakable crimes, recorded with sorrow by their own historian Gildas, they added this – that they never preached the Faith to the Saxons who dwelt among them. But God in his goodness did not utterly abandon the people whom he had chosen, for he remembered them, and sent this nation more worthy preachers of truth to bring them to the faith.[1]

Shortly after his arrival Augustine wrote a letter to Gregory asking nine questions, some of which betray his ignorance of the work of a bishop – his first question is 'What is the relationship between a bishop and his clergy?' The seventh question is 'What are to be our relations with the bishops of Gaul and Britain?' In his reply Gregory is alarmed by the suggestion that Augustine should have any authority in Gaul – 'We give you no authority over the bishops of Gaul' – but the British bishops are dealt with in two sentences: 'All the bishops of Britain, however, we commit to your charge. Use your authority to instruct the unlearned, to encourage the weak, and correct the obstinate.' There is no suggestion that Augustine might be wise to listen to them, as knowing the Anglo-Saxons a good deal better than he did. Neither is there any evidence that Gregory told the British bishops that Augustine was now their archbishop. Gregory normally writes letters with great insight and tenderness, both for those he is writing to and those he is writing about. His cursory treatment of the British bishops showed that in his mind they were under a cloud – for their failure to evangelise the Saxons, for their flirting with Pelagianism and for their strange and diverse practices. Hence his letter describes some of them as 'unlearned . . . weak . . . obstinate.'

It was not until six years after he had landed that Augustine finally met with those Gregory had put in his charge. The meeting took place at Augustine's Oak (probably near the river Severn). According to Bede, Augustine asked the British bishops to join with him in mission to the Saxons and to 'establish brotherly relations with him in Catholic unity' – which would have meant recognising him as their archbishop. They refused, and this led to a charismatic battle: a blind man was led in and the two sides were challenged to heal him. The British bishops could not but Augustine's prayers were more efficacious and the man recovered his sight. The British were discomfited and arranged a second meeting.

This time they came in strength. Seven British bishops were said to have been present, along with many 'very learned men' from 'their most famous monastery' (at Bangor-es-Coed, near Wrexham). A hermit had told the British beforehand that if Augustine courteously stood up as they approached him then 'rest assured that he is a servant of Christ'. If not, they were not to 'comply with his demands'. Augustine stayed sitting. The meeting got nowhere. It ended on a sour note with Augustine threatening that if they refused to collaborate they would be attacked by the English and killed. Bede puts a smug footnote: 'And, as if by divine judgement, all these things happened as Augustine foretold' – 1,200 of the monks from Bangor were killed.[2]

It is hardly surprising. The situation required more diplomacy than Augustine was capable of. As far as the British church leaders were concerned he was a Johnny-come-lately who had been foisted on them, who had not suffered under the Saxons as they had and who was a foreigner only able to talk to them in Latin. Above all he was asking them to renounce their traditions and adopt what they would have regarded as a new-fangled Roman pattern.

Gregory the Great's strategy

Behind the debate there stood the figure of Gregory. His strategy extended far more widely than the British Isles. He was both a reformer and a centraliser. Theologically he was an ardent disciple of Augustine of Hippo whose thought was seen as the current orthodoxy in Rome. As we have seen, and shall examine in greater detail in the next chapter, the theology of Augustine of Hippo had passed the Celtic Church by. But Gregory wanted all people to march in step with Rome. While the Celtic churches were confined to two smallish islands off the continent they could be contained, but the spread of the Celtic monasteries, through Columbanus and others, into Gaul and even Italy threatened the unity of the whole Church. Seeing it with his eyes, the need for unity in a world which was falling apart was obvious.

The differences were most obvious in liturgy, which ordinary clergy and laypeople experienced daily. Up to now each country had devised its own liturgical services within very broad limits. Gregory introduced something novel. He wanted everywhere to have the same rite – he instructed Augustine to follow the best liturgical usage: the one which he was used to in Rome, though he should allow some freedom to the English church, 'which is still new to the faith and developing as a distinct community'. Gregory was a monk, and he wanted rites for the whole Church which circled around the monastic hours. As monasticism had only comparatively recently begun to be established in the West and the Benedictine Rule was only just being introduced this was revolutionary. The fact that we still have offices derived from monastic services like Matins and Evensong in the Book of Common Prayer goes back to the reforms of Gregory and the fact that they came to be accepted throughout the Western Church. But it did not come about without opposition:

> In seventh-century Britain the struggle between the old Celtic rite and the newly introduced Roman rite was fierce. Such a struggle went on all over Western Europe ... This changeover was achieved earliest in Britain but not until the eleventh century did it even begin in Spain.[3]

Besides these differences there were divergences in church practice. Needless to say the more free-wheeling Celts did not have the precision which Rome required. They were prepared to accept ordinations by only one bishop, instead of three, while Rome would accept that only in emergencies.[4] Their preference for a church structure based upon the monastery rather than the diocese was anathema to Rome which wanted a universal pattern of dioceses governed by bishops. The Celtic subordination of bishops to abbots and, worse still, abbesses, was totally unacceptable. The Celtic priests were often married, while this was already beginning to be frowned on in Roman circles.

The central issues

In the way of such disputes two details became a focus of the division. The first was a very obvious one which would have shown immediately whether a priest was a follower of Celtic or Roman ways – the shape of the tonsure they wore. The Roman custom was to shave the crown of the head, the so-called tonsure of St Peter. The Celtic usage was to shave the head in front of the ears, calling this the tonsure of St John, the beloved disciple. The Romans jeered at the Celts, saying that they were simply copying the customs of the old pagan druids. In fact priests in many parts of the Eastern Church wore the 'St John' tonsure though possibly both sides were unaware of this.[5]

The dating of Easter was the central issue. In 444 Rome had moved over to an Alexandrian computation of the date of Easter.

The Eastern Church and the Celtic churches did not agree with this change and maintained the previous method of reckoning.[6] Needless to say this caused great confusion when the two systems of dating came into contact, for upon the date of Easter hung half the liturgical year. Exasperation with the situation which ensued when half his household was filled with Easter joy and the rest were undergoing Lenten penances seems to have been a prime factor in stimulating Oswiu to call the Synod of Whitby to sort it out.

Added to these was the accusation of Pelagianism which hung over the Celtic churches. This will be looked at further in considering the mission theology of the churches but the fact that Pelagius came from Britain and had taken the opposite side to Augustine of Hippo in a vitriolic theological dispute was enough to give an edge to the whole discussion.

The Celtic fringe

In later centuries the Romans came to see the Celts as barely semi-Christian and in the ninth century the Council of Chelsea forbade Irish priests from ministering to Anglo-Saxons. The Celtic churches were thought to be of doubtful orthodoxy, sloppy or perverse in their liturgical practice, and lacking in a scrupulous observance of canon law.

There were many areas for dispute, and it would have required a more tactful man than Augustine to make the two systems work together harmoniously. However, we have to be careful not to overemphasise the differences. Both Romans and Celts owed a common allegiance to the Pope, both shared the same Scriptures, both wanted to serve God. But in secondary matters they were far apart. In mission they often seem to have co-operated, as in East Anglia and the South of England when they came into contact. But on an official level relations were frosty.

After the fiasco of the second meeting the Irish bishops seem to have tried to effect a reconciliation between the British and Canterbury. In 610 they sent Dagan, Bishop of Inverdaoile, to Lawrence who had succeeded Augustine at Canterbury. Dagan was no backwoodsman: he had been to Rome and taken his monastic Rule to Gregory for his approval. But the meeting in Canterbury was a disaster: Dagan walked out, refusing even to sit down to eat with Lawrence. Lawrence then sent a furious letter to the Irish bishops, saying that they were no better than the recalcitrant Welsh.

The position was stalemated for many years. During the reversion to paganism in the 630s, when the Roman mission had to retreat to the South East there would have been little opportunity for contact. Only when the missionary advance of the Celtic churches meant that their practices became normal throughout England with the exception of the South East, did the need for some accommodation become urgent. Pope Honorius, who had been sufficiently interested in England to send Birinus to the West Saxons, wrote letters to the Irish church leaders asking them to conform to Roman practices and warned them 'not to imagine that their little community, isolated at the uttermost ends of the earth, had a monopoly of wisdom over all the ancient and new churches throughout the world'. A later Pope, John IV, in 640 appealed again for them to conform and added, 'We learn that the pernicious Pelagian heresy has again revived amongst you, and we strongly urge you to expel the venom of this wicked superstition from your minds.'

Wilfred and the Synod of Whitby

The Celtic churches were by no means united in their response to Rome. Some of them wanted to adopt the new Roman ways, and there was a considerable movement in that direction among the Celts before Whitby, especially in southern Ireland. A number of their leaders went wholeheartedly over to the new usage, no one more enthusiastically than Wilfred (?633–709).

Even now Wilfred polarises people. Certainly in his day he stirred people to fierce loyalty or violent opposition. He was brought up under the Celtic use at Lindisfarne. A visit to Rome in 653 converted him to the new thinking and on his return as abbot of Ripon he became a passionate reformer, introducing the Benedictine Rule and the Roman practices. He was clever, articulate, wholehearted and a thoroughgoing prelate, as far removed from the old simple style of Aidan and Cuthbert as it is possible to imagine. When he was appointed bishop he could not find in England any bishops to consecrate him whom he considered ecclesiastically satisfactory, so he went over to Gaul where the ceremony could be performed with the splendour which he considered appropriate. He was born a nobleman's son and his retinue and riches as a bishop were aristocratic. With Wilfred English prelacy was born. Even so, he could not deny his roots, for he was a fervent preacher and evangelist. In one of his many wanderings he found himself in the 680s in Sussex, one of the last pagan strongholds. He preached successfully, founded a monastery at Selsey, and had a considerable hand in bringing the faith to the area. He was apparently a brilliant speaker who spoke 'gently' and wooed his audience 'with sweet and marvellous eloquence'. His prodigious energies were not completely taken up in direct evangelism for he also improved the economy of the area by teaching the poor how to catch eels. Wilfred quarrelled with fellow-bishops and with kings and yet achieved much: an extraordinary man.

It was Wilfred, then only an abbot, who presented the Roman case at the Synod of Whitby. Summoned by King Oswiu of Northumbria in 664, the protagonists on each side gathered under his chairmanship. On the Celtic side was supposed to be the king himself, though the events of the Synod may question how loyal he was to that inheritance: he gives the impression of either being a waverer who is convinced by the argument or someone who has made his mind up beforehand. The Celts were also represented by Colman of Lindisfarne, Cedd of the East Saxons and by their hostess, Hilda. On the Roman side was the king's own son, Alchfrith. With him was Agilberht, a Frankish bishop who happened to be visiting Whitby and who had worked among the West Saxons (he was later Bishop of Paris). Also on the Roman side was old James the Deacon who had courageously stayed behind when Paulinus fled south with the remnants of Edwin's household 30 years before. Wilfred had connections with most of them for Agilberht was one of the bishops he thought fit to consecrate him and Alchfrith was a close personal friend.

Bede gives a long and comprehensive account of the Synod, though allowing much more space to the Roman arguments than to the Celtic. It is probably accurate in general if not in detail, for he would have known personally many of the people who were present.[7]

Colman put the case for the Celtic churches, citing their favourite Gospel, St John. Agilberht, as the senior churchman present, was asked to speak for the Roman side but deferred to Wilfred. Colman and Wilfred debated at length, but the argument was won conclusively when Wilfred shifted ground from discussion about the right date for Easter and asked Colman point blank: 'Is your Columba ... to take precedence before the most blessed Prince of the Apostles?' and ended by quoting 'Thou art Peter ...' from Matthew 16. It was a knockdown argument as it always had to be, for the Celts also saw themselves as loyal servants of the Pope. King Oswiu found in favour of the Romans, saying 'Peter is the guardian of the gates of heaven, and I shall not contradict him ... otherwise, when I come to the gates of heaven, he who holds the keys may not be willing to open them.'

Whether Whitby was as important nationally as Bede says is doubtful, for it can be seen as little more than a gathering of Northumbrian bishops with a few visitors. The *Anglo-Saxon Chronicle* for the year does not even mention it, though it does record the subsequent departure of Colman for Iona. It is not difficult to see it as already stitched up in advance: the king's son played a prominent part, and many of the people on the Roman side had connections with Wilfred. But whether it was engineered or not, there is no doubt that the central argument was obedience to the See of Peter, and given the presuppositions of all present, there was never any doubt what the verdict would be. From the start of the discussion the Celts were on the back foot, for it was inevitably a rearguard action when many of their own people were adopting the new ways.

It may have been a turning point: it was certainly a milestone. For Bede it was decisive for after Whitby he treats everyone who did not immediately conform as contumacious. Archbishop Theodore of Canterbury (d. 690) was more conciliatory and in 672 held the Synod of Hertford, which tried to make the path of reconciliation easier. However, it is clear that relationships between those who still followed the Celtic pattern and those who were Roman became increasingly bitter. In 705 Bishop Aldhelm of Sherborne complained that the Welsh clergy 'will neither pray with us in church, nor eat with us at table'.

Most of the clergy slowly adopted the Roman usages – except

the Welsh who remained defiant for centuries. Iona first celebrated the Roman Easter in 716. For the monasteries the growth of the diocesan pattern of working and the widespread adoption of the Benedictine Rule meant that abbots and abbesses were no longer superior to bishops, but the relationship between a community and its local bishop caused many headaches down the centuries and difficulties are not unknown even today.

The bishop

The early bishops were evangelists. Whether Roman or Celtic they saw their prime task as bringing the gospel to the pagans, baptising them into Christ and bringing them up in the faith. Soon, however, the need to administer a diocese, to keep up with the riches of the court, to behave as a Roman gentleman, changed the work and the attitude of the episcopate. Previously the bishop spent much of his time walking through the villages preaching and baptising. Now he only had time to make occasional forays from his position beside the king. In Wilfred we can see one whose extraordinary energy was able to combine the two, for he was both an evangelist and also a potentate. He evangelised heartily whenever he had the chance, but he came from an Anglo-Saxon background which cared greatly about outward show. The artefacts they put in graves, and their literature, show that they believed in conspicuous consumption. It is not surprising that in contrast to the meagre possessions left by Bede on his death, Wilfred left behind him gold and gems and much silver and something akin to an 'ecclesiastical empire'.[8] The change was probably inevitable, though it was one which Bede himself regretted.

The type of bishop changed. The king now had a major influence on the appointment of those who were to be his advisers and when this was allied to the changes in the monasteries brought about by the coming of the Benedictine Rule, it meant that the safe and predictable came to be preferred to the unusual and charismatic.

The people who found Christ, had found their demon-ridden world become beneficent and they were grateful. Alongside this was the tradition that kings and the aristocracy were generous givers. When Caedwalla conquered the Isle of Wight he promised (before his baptism) to give a quarter to Wilfred who had brought him to Christ. As a result the Church rapidly became very rich. The austerity of the early saints was replaced by an easier lifestyle, their mud and wattle huts by substantial buildings. This had considerable economic repercussions. Across the Channel as early as the sixth century a Frankish king was complaining that 'all our wealth is the hands of bishops; our honour perishes'.

By 700 villages were making a *tributum* – a tithe to the coffers of the Church in return for spiritual care; Bede complained that the ordinary people often gave much and received little. Coupled with the 'tax dodge' whereby monasteries and later parish churches could be treated as tax-free zones, the Church grew richer still. But riches never improve a church and few are able to resist their degrading effect.

Diocese and parish

The diocesan pattern which Gregory had in mind when he sent Augustine was based on the twelve Roman administrative areas which had fallen apart 200 years before, and he wanted archbishoprics in each of the old Roman provinces at London and York. As we have seen, a diocese was soon established at London but it had to be abandoned because of the reversion to paganism in 616 and Mellitus, its first bishop, was forced to leave. As a result, the southern province has an Archbishop in Canterbury, rather than the more obvious London, to this day. When Paulinus went north he tried to establish himself in York but seems to have done little except build a church there (or restore a Roman-British church) before he too was forced to flee before resurgent paganism in 633.

The Celts looked after people: the Romans looked after an area. The contrast is often made but is only partially true. While the invasions were happening and people were moving from place to place, and while a basically tribal social structure was normal, then Celtic forms of ministry were more effective. It used small groups of highly motivated Christians to minister to each tribe and grouping. For peoples on the move the pilgrim form of ministry was most appropriate, for spontaneity and flexibility were the most important requirements.

However, once the tribe grew into a more settled kingdom and the Christian group had settled down in a substantial monastery, the advantages of the Celtic pattern became less obvious. If villages were paying *tributum* then they wanted more than occasional visits from a cleric. Coupled with this was the growth in power and significance of the nobility. Initially they were warriors gathered around the king to protect and fight for him. Now they were being given parcels of land, as the rash of written charters from this period attest.

They were the *nouveaux riches* of their day and they wanted their wealth to be visible. As part of this they wanted their own churches and their own clergy. In still pagan Scandinavia nobles owned their own temples and performed their own sacrifices. The Anglo-Saxon nobleman followed this and saw the parish church as his own property – to be sold, destroyed or left by will to whoever he pleased. Often, for convenience to himself but possibly a long way from the village, he built the church as a chapel attached to his hall. He also wanted to appoint his own priest who would be chaplain to his household as well as priest to the parish. These rights of patronage hardened into legal property and are with us still.

In the old days the Celtic Christians gathered for worship around the high crosses which were dotted around the country-side. But even the Celts were beginning to meet in simple churches of wattle and daub, and the high crosses were not replicated in England after the conversion. Further, many monasteries had degenerated into tax-evasion exercises run by local landowners. All too soon the idealism of the early days was lost in the social and ecclesiastical pressures which was pushing towards a parish church with a priest in every place. It was probably inevitable in a more settled environment, but there was a half-way house which can teach us much.

As the early missionary bishops with their support team of priests and laypeople settled near a king's court they began to see the main church as a missionary centre from which to thrust out into the surrounding countryside. These 'minsters' were semi-monastic mother churches with a strong evangelistic emphasis on planting churches and Christian communities in the surrounding area. Usually the bishop, rather than an abbot, was in charge, and from a minster a wide area could be ministered to by his clergy and lay team, evangelising the places which were still pagan and caring for those areas which had become Christian. As these major churches evolved, some of them became the place where the bishop's chair was placed and this was the starting point for many of our present-day cathedrals. The minster was a half-way house between the monastic mission of the Celts and the parochial system, and it deserves to be looked at again today.

As more settled times came, once the invasions were over and before the Vikings swarmed across the landscape, the parish system began to be slowly established. It is often described as the work of Archbishop Theodore, and certainly much of his work was involved with setting the system in place. The Synod of Hertford in 672 pressed the English Church firmly in the direction of the parish system and away from the Celtic pattern. However it was a very slow process, barely complete by the time of the Norman Conquest four centuries later.

In part the shortage of priests was to blame. At the time of the conversion their number can never have been great: 30 was the canonical age at which a man could be ordained priest, and when the short life span of people in the seventh century is considered, their ministerial life was bound to be limited. It was only when the nobility demanded large numbers of clergy to man their parish churches that a greater number was produced. They were little better educated than the peasantry, for they were made responsible for their churches and given a small acreage of glebe land in order to support themselves. Like the peasants they were subservient to their lord and had to obey him. The bishop became a shadowy figure with an exceedingly large diocese, in an age of slow transport. If it came to a difference of opinion between their lord and their bishop there was little doubt who had the most immediate impact.

Notes

1   *Ecclesiastical History* 1.22 – Gildas was an excitable Welsh monk who wrote *c.* 550. He saw things in black and white terms with a strong apocalyptic flavour and, in the way of such people, saw the Anglo-Saxon invasions and the defeat of the British as God's vengeance upon the sins of the people he was addressing. Bede took him at face value.

2   *Ecclesiastical History* 2.2.

3   George Guiver, *Company of Voices* (1988).

4 Gregory gave permission to Augustine to consecrate alone and Paulinus was left in a similar situation as the only bishop in England when two bishops were drowned on their way from Rome.

5 This is comically illustrated in the appointment of Theodore as Archbishop. In 666 an archbishop-elect had been brought from England for confirmation by the Pope, but no sooner had he arrived in Rome than he died. Following the Synod of Whitby and a severe outbreak of the plague, the Church in England needed firm leadership; there was no time to send back to England for another candidate, so Pope Vitalian had to find another archbishop. He approached Hadrian and others but they all refused. Eventually he asked the aged Theodore, a monk from Tarsus (possibly ejected by the advancing Muslims) to take the job. He accepted and was ordained sub-deacon, priest and bishop within a few months. However, as an Eastern monk he had the 'St John' tonsure, which would have been politically catastrophic, so he had to wait for four months until his hair grew sufficiently to be given an orthodox Roman haircut. Eventually, accompanied by Hadrian and Benedict Biscop he set out, arriving in England in 669, aged 67. One wonders what the English Church made of him, or how soon Vitalian expected to be having to find another Archbishop of Canterbury. In fact he had 21 years of ministry and was one of the most significant archbishops between Augustine and Lanfranc – a great example for the chronologically challenged.

6 Some of the Eastern Orthodox churches still have their own calendar.

7 *Ecclesiastical History* 3.25.

8 R. H. Hodgkin, *A History of the Anglo-Saxons* (1952).

Chapter 9

The Theology of Mission

The unseen link with Byzantium

In Ireland and other places influenced by the Celtic churches there are standing crosses, often wondrously carved. Some show biblical scenes intended to be a teaching aid, while others have complex interweavings which are a sinuous expression of the praise of God. As Ian Bradley says, 'They weren't meant to be talked about in terms of aesthetics but to symbolise Christ and the Crucifixion. They were put up literally to stop people in their tracks.'[1]

To see their like you have to cross Europe into Moldavia. Many of the people in and around the Black Sea are of Celtic origin – in Galatia, St Paul may have heard Celtic spoken as the native language. Even today there are strong linguistic connections between Irish and some languages of Turkey and Romania. The reason is that the Celts were an ancient people who had covered most of northern Europe in their time, their heyday being the last centuries before Christ. Then (to simplify a complex process) they had been squeezed – from the south by the growing power of Rome and from the north by Germanic invaders. They had split into two halves, part pressed into modern Romania and Turkey, while the western part was concentrated into the British Isles, Spain and western Gaul.

But the links between the Celts of East and West are more than archaeological and linguistic. There were also links of theology and practice. Neither Byzantium nor the Celtic churches of the West had fallen under the spell of Augustine of Hippo, whose writings and outlook had come to dominate the Church at Rome. In part political factors were at work. In the East the Church had been steadily asserting its independence of Rome, and church leaders in Constantinople, the leading city of the Mediterranean world, could only look down on the Bishop of Rome, a spiritual leader of a city which had declined to the second rank and was sinking lower still. Constantinople could at least boast that it still had an empire, and emperors of the standing of Justinian could claim that they were the true successors of the emperors of Rome. The Byzantine dream was 'of a universal Christian society administered by the emperor and spiritually guided by the Church' – they spiritualised it by saying that the emperor and the church were like the two natures of Christ, a 'symphony'.[2] It was a vision in direct conflict with that of Gregory I.

In the West the Irish Church and its offshoots retained some links with Rome, but the troubled conditions of the fifth and sixth centuries meant that the nuances of theological ideas could not easily be transmitted. The heresies which convulsed the Roman Church were merely far off murmurs in Ireland, and the Celtic churches had gone their own way, working out their own theology. Besides this they were thought to have their own particular heresy. Although Pelagius was a Briton, he spent nearly all his active life in the Mediterranean area and probably never returned to his homeland. Nevertheless Pelagianism was closely identified with Britain and suspicions of its continuance lasted long into succeeding centuries: Romans were still accusing the Celts of harbouring an attachment to it as late as the ninth century. Pelagianism will be examined more below but the heresy was at its peak at the beginning of the fifth century as Rome struggled to impose orthodoxy upon the churches which owed allegiance to it.

The links between the far East and the far West of the Christian world were strengthened by the monastic tradition which came to be so dominant in Ireland. This was long before the Benedictine pattern became universal in the British Isles and the earlier links had been with Eastern monasticism, sometimes direct and sometimes via St Martin of Tours. If we wish to understand the theology of Ireland we need to look at least as much to contemporary Byzantine theology as to that of Rome. There was also a common determination not to be bullied into a slavish following of the Roman pattern, whether this was the latest liturgical fancy or the dating of Easter. Constantinople and the Celts were at one in this, though as far as can be known there was no direct communi-

cation between the two elements within the Church. It would
have enormously strengthened the hand of Colman and the other
upholders of the Celtic tradition at Whitby if they could have
cited other churches which held to non-Roman ways, but they
did not appear to do so.

Mission theologies

The mission theology which the Celtic churches used in their
evangelization, first of Scotland and then of England and the
Continent, was partly imported, partly home-brewed.

Reading through the Celtic writings one is constantly made
aware of the fact that for them theology was not a subject for study
but an expression of faith. It was from their personal experience of
the three persons of the Trinity that they came to make that
understanding of the Christian faith central to their thinking and
their praying. It was from the beauty of the world around them
and their awareness of the goodness of which human beings are
capable that they came to proclaim the basic optimism of the
Christian message – and this was to be very different from
the Roman attitude. It was because of their personal experience
of the struggle to be a Christian that they came to understand
temptation, not as a psychological phenomenon but as the mos-
quitoes sent by the devil to bite and harry the human race. It was
because of their understanding of the continuity of their history
that, when considering the paganism from which they had turned,
they were less ready to wipe the slate clean and start again than
were those from Rome with their brisk 'let's start things from
scratch' attitude.

There is a tendency today to overemphasise the differences
between Celtic and Roman theology, often so that the writers can
impose their own preferences upon the reader. There certainly
were different theological nuances, but the differences of theological approach and attitude were greater.

The theology brought to England by Augustine of Canterbury
was up to date, well thought through, a cohesive schema – very
Roman in its style. Gregory the Great stood at the pinnacle of
several centuries of Christian learning, during which orthodoxy
had thrown aside heresy after heresy – Sabellianism, Nestorianism,

Monophysitism – and the most widespread of all, Arianism. In doing so it had become more precise and intellectually coherent, but it had inevitably lost some of its soul. The poetry had gone out of it. Verbal definitions had become its substance and assent to these was replacing a personal faith in the Triune God. Theology had become a subject to be studied rather than an explanation of a life to be lived; orthodoxy ('right belief') was becoming more important than orthopraxis ('right practice'). Augustine of Hippo had summed it all up magnificently, and had himself engaged robustly with Pelagianism, one of the last of the great heresies before Gregory's time, but his heirs tended to copy his words rather than his passion for the gospel.

Eastern Orthodoxy has never allowed the divorce between prayer and theology to become so wide. For the East the faith is not susceptible to exact definition for it has always believed that at the heart of faith there is mystery. So there has never been an Eastern Aquinas who could sum up the whole of Christian truth in measured tones, and even today it would be impossible for there to be a summary of Orthodox teaching like the 1,300 pages of the modern *Cathechism of the Catholic Church*. For the Orthodox, not everything has to be reduced to words and definitions: some things can only be expressed in silence or adoration.

It is a pity that the Orthodox methods of theology were not followed in the great debate which racked the Mediterranean church in the early fifth century, for it illustrates only too well the dangers of being too precise, too verbal and not being prepared to acknowledge the limits of human knowledge.

Pelagianism

Those enamoured of Celtic ways in the 'Green Industry' have espoused the cause of Pelagius, and contrasted it with a black Augustinianism. Others have seen it as a peculiarly British disease. Karl Barth called British theology 'incurably Pelagian', and the name of Pelagius has been used as a theological put down for centuries. Recent studies have shown that Pelagius' theology was a good deal more subtle and more influential than had been thought.[3]

Alongside these second thoughts about his theology, there has been growing disquiet about the thinking of his great (and victorious) adversary, Augustine of Hippo. Writers taking the Celtic viewpoint are scathing: 'The pessimism and anti-humanism of the later Augustine has cast a chilling gloom across Western Christendom.'[4] The dispute concerning the place of human free will and the grace of God is still not settled, and recent claims about the influence of our genetic inheritance and sociological experience mean that it is not likely to be resolved soon. How far can human beings be really said to be free? To be free means being able to make choices – otherwise such human concepts as responsibility and duty, and ethical concepts such as right and wrong, become largely meaningless. Whether we speak as theologians about the irresistible grace of God, as sociologists about the shaping force of nurturing experience or as biologists about genetic determinism is almost immaterial. If we are robots, pre-programmed to make a certain choice at a certain time, then we can carry neither guilt or blame. Whether we are criminals or saints is not because of either our depravity or our goodness but is in our genes or our environment, and so it is no more blameworthy than having red hair or speaking a certain language.

While Pelagius was of course unaware of modern notions of determinism, he was unhappy with the moral effect that he thought he perceived in Augustine's emphasis on divine election. If God has chosen us whether we liked it or not and whether we were good or bad, then we may as well act as we please because we are not responsible for our actions.[5]

The three great controversialists in the dispute were contemporaries. Pelagius was born c. 350 in Britain, Jerome c. 341 in Dalmatia and Augustine c. 354 in Algeria. By the 380s they were together in Rome. Augustine had given up his dissolute past and been magnificently converted, Jerome was beginning his great translation of the Bible and Pelagius was a learned layperson (it is often said that Pelagius was a monk, but the evidence for this is very uncertain and it is likely that he was a lay spiritual guide and scholar). For the next twenty years Pelagius remained in Rome, appalled by the low standards of morality, and preaching a modified asceticism. The arguments began just after the turn of the century. Augustine began to proclaim what Pelagius thought was a dangerous departure from the Christian tradition.

Augustine had been overwhelmed by the goodness of the God who had revealed himself and brought him to faith. He felt he had been led into false teaching by the Manichaeans who saw a black vs. white universe where the good God fought the evil God, but now the true God had shown him the light of Christ. For nine years he had been bound by false teaching but now he was free. It seemed to him as though he had no part in the process; it had all been God's doing, and his *Confessions* emphasise this. He could echo the Pauline cry, 'It is by grace you are saved through faith: it is not your own doing. It is God's gift, not a reward for work done'.[6] Pelagius protested that something must be left to human response: it could not all be God's responsibility or the moral universe collapsed in determinism.

Augustine spelt out in more detail than had previously been attempted the doctrine of original sin. When Adam sinned the stain of that deed passed to all his successors; and the means of that passing was 'concupiscence'. Augustine was not so banal as to equate concupiscence with sexual intercourse. For him it was everything which centred upon the created rather than the Creator: he lists pride, avarice, theft, sacrilege etc., but, all the same, sexual desire (*concupiscentia carnis*) was its prominent manifestation.

This link between original sin and sex was to have sad consequences. Jerome, now in Jerusalem, was becoming more and more shrill in his teaching that virginity is a more excellent way than marriage. Jerome's view of women was not flattering – the only means of spiritual growth for them was for them to become honorary men: 'If a woman wants to serve Christ more than the world, she will cease to be a woman, and will be called man because we want all the perfect to be exalted to become man.' While Augustine did not take so extreme a position he began to see sexual desire as the main channel whereby Adam's taint passed from generation to generation. This had practical consequences which as a bishop he had to enforce: since he saw baptism as cancelling Adam's legacy of original sin, it was important that babies should be baptised as soon as possible – otherwise they would be damned.

Pelagius was aghast. While in Rome he had condemned the fatalism of the Manichees who saw the human soul as the battlefield for external spiritual forces. In Augustine's insistence that babies were born in sin without personal fault he found the same rejection of personal responsibility. He passionately refuted Augustine's pessimistic assessment of the human condition. He wrote and he taught for, as an intellectual, he firmly believed that all that was required was good teaching:[7] good Bible teaching and a knowledge of the commandments. Like 'Disgusted of Tunbridge Wells' he insisted on good moral teaching – and hefty punishment for those who disobeyed, for he was a strict and by no means a lenient moralist: 'In the day of judgement no forbearance will be shown to the ungodly and the sinners but they will be consumed in eternal fires.'

Augustine fought back, and he had the big guns on his side. By 410 the divisions were complete. The earlier courteous tone in which the debate had been conducted hardened and Pelagius and his followers began to be condemned by church councils and synods. With each succeeding year Augustine produced more extreme diatribes against the Pelagians and it is from these darker later years that we find the insistence on predestination and double predestination – the teaching that some are chosen by God for salvation and others chosen by God for damnation. By the time of Augustine's death in 430 the Pelagians were a small and fleeing group, and teachers were being despatched from Rome to fumigate those areas which had been worst infected.

One of these areas was Britain. It appears that Pelagianism had entered Britain in 420 through the teaching of Agricola, the son of a Continental bishop. Palladius was sent in 431 to Ireland and Germanus was sent to England some years later to extirpate the heresy, but there was little other indication of Pelagianism in Britain, though it was a useful stick with which to beat the Celtic Church.

Was the Celtic Church Pelagian?

How far then was Celtic Christianity Pelagian? The disputes happened far away in Italy and the Middle East and Pelagius appears to have died in Egypt c. 424.

It is impossible to ignore the political backdrop. In 410 the barbarians were not at the gates – they were within the city. Rome was sacked by the Vandals, Pelagius himself had fled as a refugee before the onslaught in 409. Augustine was writing letters to clergy advising them whether they should stay with their people or get out. He died in 430 in a city besieged by the Vandals. We may joke about 'the end of civilisation as we know it', but for the Roman Empire of those days it was sober truth. Only in the East and a few parts of North Africa was the old Roman administration still in place.

It is within that situation that we need to evaluate Pelagianism in Britain. The last Roman troops had left. The Saxons and the Jutes and the Angles had blocked the easiest route to Rome. Gaul was in turmoil. For a century the British Isles were adrift. Communication with the Continent of Europe became extremely difficult. A few monks and priests escaped from Gaul and brought news, but the British Christians were on their own. The theological disputes of Rome were no more than the far off rumblings. The Celtic Church went on its way with what would come to be regarded in Rome as a rather old-fashioned theology and out-of-date liturgical practices. It was not that Britain took Pelagius to its heart; rather that it did not take Augustine of Hippo into its thinking. And Augustine had preached a curiously modern psychological gospel. He was interested in what went on in his head: hence the questions about free will and faith which bothered him. The Celts were left with a more objective 'external' gospel. Sin was not so much something to do with what happened inside a person as the attacks of Satan from outside. Faith was shown objectively by asceticism and prayer rather than subjectively in a battle between doubt and trust. One suspects that even if they ever heard a whisper of what was the latest theological theory, they would not have been impressed.

For the Celtic churches their most influential spokesman appeared centuries later. John Scotus Erigena (John the Irishman') was born in Ireland in the ninth century and spent much of his life at Laon in France. He was a true Celt, for his theology is infused with poetry and the visionary element is strong. Significantly his teachings were condemned in 855 as 'Scot's porridge' at the Synod of Valence; there seem to have been two charges against him – a denial of the reality of hell and a belief in pantheism. It is significant that these were the areas of greatest dispute with Pelagius four centuries before and they are still debated today.

One of his works which survives is *On Predestination* (written c. 865), in which he finds the Augustinian thesis that every child is damned to hell until and unless it is baptised totally repugnant. Even worse for him is the Augustinian double predestination. In his best known work *De Divisione Naturae*, he tackled the heart of the problem: is the Christian view of the world to be optimistic or pessimistic? If it is essentially evil, then creation is to be beaten into submission to the will of God. If it is good, it is to be worked with and honoured as something sacramental, in which we can see the hand of the one who created it. If a pessimistic view is taken, then the Church is an ark into which to drag as many souls as possible so that they may be saved from the final bonfire. If the view taken is optimistic, then the Church prays that God's Kingdom 'may come on earth as it does in heaven', and co-operates with nature. It is a fundamental distinction. In the heat of debate and with a darkening political world around him, Augustine of Hippo took too pessimistic a view to be biblical. This was compounded by his emphasis on the sexual act as being the main way in which sin was transmitted from one generation to another. The material world became so infused with sin that it should be avoided as much as possible and not seen as a delight and a gift of God. Further, the sexual act should only be used for procreation – and this has social, economic and ecclesiastical ramifications even today in the arguments which lie behind the Roman Catholic refusal to use any except 'natural' contraception.

Like Orthodoxy, the Celtic churches were intensely biblical. As you look at one of the early Northumbrian manuscripts you can see that through his artistry the copyist was expressing his deep love of the Scriptures and reverence for them. Monasteries reverberated with the sound of the Bible being sung and being recited – and muttered, for most readers mouthed the words even when alone. One painstaking scholar has computed that in Patrick's brief *Confession* and his *Letter to Coroticus* (written to a British prince, whose soldiers were mistreating Christian converts) there are 340 quotations from 46 different books of the Bible.

But the way in which they interpreted the Bible was different from Augustine. There is a suspicion that Augustine in his later years drifted back to the dualistic Manichaeism which he had found so attractive at one point in his life. This derivation from

Persian thinking divided human existence into the physical life and the spiritual. The world around us is bad, the inner life of the spirit is good. Certainly in some of his later writings Augustine sees creation as so contaminated by sin that it is to be avoided. The Celts would have none of this. For them the world was beautiful and men and women capable of great good. For Augustine even the beauty of the world is spoilt in some measure by sin, for creation is intrinsically corrupt. The Eastern Christians were more optimistic, wanting us to see the creation as indeed subject to sin, but capable of liberation. This applied even to human beings, and the Byzantine theologians expressed this in terms of 'deification' – they constantly refer to the words of Irenaeus, 'If the Word has been made man, it is so that men may be made gods'. Deification is the goal of every Christian, and Eastern theologians often pick up the Pauline teaching that a Christian is 'adopted' as a child of God. Thus St Symeon the New Theologian, writing a century after John Erigena, says 'he who is God by nature [i.e. God himself] converses with those whom he has made gods by grace, as a friend converses with his friends, face to face'.[8]

This does not mean that the Celts forgot or downplayed the redemptive side of Christianity. The extreme mortifications of the flesh they subjected themselves to, standing for hours in prayer with arms outstretched, eating only meagre rations, enduring sleeplessness and hard work, show that they took sin with all seriousness. The cross was pivotal to their theology. On the Celtic crosses they carved the circle of the sun to represent nature, but central to the whole was the symbol of the crucifixion. They did not follow Pelagius, who in the heat of the argument went too far and began to see sin as of little importance. They were only too well aware of its existence and all-pervading character. For them the attacks of the devil were all too real, for the Celts lived in a world awhirl with angels and demons. On the cross Christ won victory over all the powers of darkness, and the work of the Church was to resist the enemy and live in the peace and light of Christ.

'Christus Victor' (Christ the Victor) was the triumphant Saviour from all the powers of hell. He was the protector, and the 'circle prayers' ask for the shield of the cross against the demons 'who prowl and prowl around'. Typically, the Celts had no worked out doctrine – for them the cross spoke of freedom and protection and peace rather than of any 'theory of the atonement'.

Some modern authors have tried to suggest that they emphasised the incarnation at the expense of the atonement. Some writers say this with disapproval – those who are trying to tar the Celts with a New Age brush. Others approve – those who see the Celts as children of the dawn gently speaking of a universal God who loves all and judges nobody. One suspects that a Celtic monastery would not have recognised that caricature, any more than a Roman monastery would have recognised the hard-nosed image which is sometimes wished upon them. All the evidence points to the fact that the Celts were thoroughly orthodox, but their theology was akin to that of the Eastern Church and the fourth century rather than that of the Augustinian model, which had been so persuasive in Rome and which made all before it seem rather old-fashioned and incoherent.

The Celtic message

We have no way of hearing the voice of the Celtic preachers as they went into the villages and spoke before the kings and chieftains. Unconsciously their hagiographers tell us more about themselves than their subjects. We have a few shafts of light, though we have no way of knowing whether they were typical. Nevertheless we can infer something of the pattern of their preaching.

In a pagan world which was crowded with superstitions and where fate was seen as the inexorable force which wove human destinies, the first message seems to have been one of a God who was in control and a God who willed their good. Instead of a pantheon of gods who were trying to fight or love or trick each other, there was the ordered pattern of the Trinity, three persons in harmony and unity.

The Being of God was central to their preaching. In place of the confused multitude of gods they spoke of the communal unity of the Trinity, the Alone who is not alone, the social individual. The *perichoresis*, the mutual interpenetration of the persons of the Trinity, is symbolised for them in the convolutions of the Celtic knot. They ransacked their everyday experience to express this truth:

Three folds of the cloth, yet only one napkin is there,
Three joints of the finger, yet still only one finger fair,
Three leaves of the shamrock, yet no more than one shamrock to
    wear,
Frost, snow-flakes and ice, all in water their origin share,
Three persons in God, to one God alone we make our prayer.

The world they lived in was often a threatening place, with natural forces ranged against them – their poetry speaks much of the bitter cold of winter, the uncertainty of the harvests, the threatening gloom of the forests, the shortness of human life. The new preachers spoke of the one God who made it all and controlled it all; no longer was one god apportioned to the forests and another to the seas and another to the fertility of the land. The preachers showed that God was sovereign throughout the world. Patrick presented God as 'the God of heaven and earth, of sea and river, of sun and moon and stars, of the lofty mountain and the lowly valley, the God above heaven, the God in heaven, the God under heaven'.

The pagan world was unbelievably complicated: myth piled on myth so that even today we cannot find coherence or a unifying theme. How much more confusing it must have been for the peasant or the illiterate king trying to hold together the highly coloured but often conflicting stories of the gods which they heard from their skalds. The ordinary human being felt caught up among supernatural forces which he could control only by magic spells and rituals.

A gospel for all

Paganism was the faith of a heroic society. The gods were on the side of the big battalions, and when victory was won you showed your gratitude by making sacrifices to the appropriate god – often using your prisoners as sacrificial material. Christianity portrayed a more gentle society where poor people were valued as well as rich, where God was seen as being as interested in those who were never invited into the king's hall as in those who were welcome within it. The Celtic bishop Fastidius spoke of the social implications of the gospel in 411: 'A Christian is a man who . . . never allows a poor man to be oppressed when he is by, whose door is open to all, whose table every poor man knows, whose food is offered to all.'

This was not mere rhetoric. The early saints lived out their preaching. The holy Aidan, first Bishop of Lindisfarne, is described by Bede as 'a man of the greatest gentleness, godliness and moderation'. Typically the only thing that Bede thought was wrong with him was that 'he was accustomed to observe the day of the Lord's Easter according to the manner of his nation'. As we have seen, this depth of Christian commitment was even true of the kings whose profession of faith was so influential that some of them in later life entered a monastery in order to follow the way of Christ more faithfully.

A rock in a dangerous world

The Christian faith spoke of stability and order and peace. For many it must have been like a drink of clear, cool water after the superheated spiritual atmosphere of the pagan gods. The preachers told how they could cope with the forces of evil by the cross of Christ, spoke of worship as centred upon one God, not many, and invited them to a simple rite of baptism.

Baptism was the crucial sacrament of commitment. In the circumstances of those days a private baptism was almost impossible. It had to be a public renunciation of one faith and the acceptance of another. Often it was in the local river and there would have been crowds of people clustered around. The scene must have been reminiscent of John the Baptist at the river Jordan – and some of the early preachers had more than a touch of the personal force of John the Baptist, for they must have been imposing individuals with some of the demeanour of an Old Testament prophet. Even the gentle Aidan 'was a master of the stern word and the frightening prophecy'.[9]

Mass baptism seems to have been common, with hundreds being baptised at a time. In a world where people lived in communities so close that it was difficult to marry without committing incest, the value of having a whole community baptised into Christ was obvious. As in many missionary situations today, the impact of community baptisms must have been startling. The effect on the individuals concerned must have varied: for some it expressed their new found faith, for others it was just another belief to add to what they knew, while many must have just followed along confused and mystified. But perhaps more important than the faith of the individuals concerned, the action symbolised a change in the community, for thenceforth the Church would have been central to the community and children would have been brought up in the faith.

At times the coming of the Christian faith has broken families and communities, drawing individuals out of their existing networks into a new one which supersedes all others. This is an inevitable consequence when individuals find Christ one by one. However it does not always have to be so. Whether they came from the Celtic or the Roman tradition, the preachers to the Anglo-Saxons offered them the opportunity of remaining together as a community as they walked together into the waters of baptism, together experienced release from the forces around them, together joined in the new worship which they hardly understood and together adapted the old pagan temple or built their new church. Faith strengthened community rather than breaking it. Once the king had legitimised the process by his own conversion, or acquiesced in the proclamation of the faith, this must have been what conversion meant as village after village accepted the faith.

We know that the old ways died hard. Some habits were given a Christian twist so that the old pagan festivals became Christian feasts, just as the old standing stones with their phallic significance were 'christianised' by having the cross of Christ or the chi-rho symbol carved on them. The missionaries tried to ensure that the jolt when a community becomes Christian should be as slight as possible. Thus in giving advice about the status of the old pagan temples once an area had become Christian, Gregory sounds more like an archdeacon than a pope in his concern for the practical as well as the spiritual: 'If the temples are well-built they are to be purified from devil-worship, and dedicated to the service of the true God.' He recognised that people would more easily come to a familiar building rather than a new one so that they, 'seeing that their temples are not destroyed, may abandon idolatry and resort to these places as before, and may come to know and adore the true God'.

Gregory wanted evangelism to cause as few ripples as possible in the socio-economic field. A king would not thank the Christians if they caused division in his kingdom, separated his subjects into groups and aroused a fierce opposition. Above all a king who was upset would not allow the faith to be preached or be converted himself. It was because of the need for the sacral king to preserve the unity and peace of his kingdom that Edwin was understandably anxious to get the agreement of his counsellors to the new faith, and why Oswiu was concerned enough to convene the Synod of Whitby when division did occur. Neither Roman nor Celtic missionaries needlessly stirred up opposition, and the 'conversion' produced no martyrs – it is all rather unheroic, but it was effective. Some modern evangelists who calculate their effectiveness on the amount of opposition that is around may need to take note.

Today

As we have seen in Chapter 4 the 'new evangelism' has swung rapidly towards a non-Augustinian view of the world, for it has found that people outside the life of the Church are interested, even fascinated, by the being of God. Conversely it has been found that people have little or no sense of personal guilt, let alone a sense of sin towards a holy God.[10] Thus the Celtic/Byzantine acceptance of the basic wonder and glory of the creation chimes in well with modern ecological concerns, and their exultation in the Triune God is in accord with a generation which is well prepared to accept mystery and paradox.

In ten thousand catechumenate and nurture groups they preach unwittingly a Celtic/Byzantine gospel: 'Let us together explore who God is and see where the journey takes us.'

Notes

1 *The Celtic Way* (1993).
2 John Meyendorff, *Byzantine Theology* (1974).
3 Cf. Rees *Pelagius: A Reluctant Hero* (1988); Evans, *Pelagius: Inquiries and*

Reappraisals (1968); De Bruyn, *Pelagius' Commentary on St Paul's Epistle to the Romans* (1993).

4 Donoghue, *Aristocracy of Soul: Patrick of Ireland* (1987).
5 St Paul faces the same criticism in Romans 6.
6 Ephesians 2.8f (REB).
7 Some books still say that we know nothing of Pelagius apart from what we hear from his adversaries. In fact there are seven extant publications and fragments of eleven others.
8 There are similarities with the 'perfectionism' which John Wesley preached and which is part of the Methodist inheritance.
9 James Campbell, *Essays in Anglo-Saxon History* (1986).
10 Cf. John Finney, *Finding Faith Today* (1992).

Chapter 10

The Seventh Century and God

Celt, Anglo-Saxon, Roman

There was a great famine over the land of Sweden. In the first year of dearth they sacrificed oxen; in the second year they sacrificed human beings; in the third year 'they all agreed that the time of famine was on account of their king' – and so Domaldi of Sweden was killed. The sacral king was sacrificed for the good of the nation.

The Anglo-Saxon gods were tempestuous, demanding, unpredictable and to be placated. When king Oswald, who had revived the faith again in Northumbria, was killed on 5 August 642 by the inevitable Penda, his head and arms and hands were hacked off and hung on a tree as an offering to Woden. Woden was 'the hanging god' and sacrifices to him were traditionally hung on a tree and stabbed by a spear; early evangelists did not hesitate to make the obvious comparison to the crucifixion, and used it in their preaching.

We know less of the beliefs of the Celts before they were converted, but the druidic religion seems to have tried to come to terms with the uncertainties of life and the threats of the natural world through hidden wisdoms and arcane learning. It sought to placate the natural forces of creation by magic and worship of the gods of the wood and water. We know few of their myths since they forbade the use of writing. Yet many modern writers, in spite of minimal historical evidence, describe the ancient druidic faith as ecologically sound, unconcerned by gender and having an air of sweet reasonableness. There is little or no historical evidence to support these assertions. Archaeological remains are sparse and ambiguous, Christian writings give no more than oblique references and we have to rely on comments on druidic religion made centuries earlier and often half a continent away. The religion of the Celtic lands at the time of the Christian missions is almost unknown – intelligent guesses about the meaning of a meagre handful of facts is the best we can do.

Thus it is often confidently asserted that the Celtic soul friend or spiritual guide (Irish: *anamchara*) is a Christianization of the druidic counsellor which Celtic chieftains had. That may be true but the Eastern Church provides an alternative source of the idea, for the Greek *syncellus* ('the one who shares a cell') had the same function. Remembering the Celtic links with Eastern monasteries, the latter is at least as probable.

This is not to say that the previous religion is unimportant. The background of paganism left its mark on the Christianity which succeeded it: the historical difficulty is to distinguish those elements which came from the culture of the past from those which came from other traditions and from those which were new minted by a creative people. Apart from a situation where there has been ethnic cleansing it is never possible totally to wipe out a culture and on that *tabula rasa* to imprint another. Culture is too deep rooted, too all-pervasive in human society to change overnight: it can be altered but never destroyed. Christianity is many-hued. The cloth may be that of the gospel, but the colours it is dyed come from the cultures which embrace it. Indian Christianity will never be the same as that of Europe, or that of China the same as that of South America. In the same way the Celtic culture coloured the gospel one colour and the Anglo-Saxon another. But that was not the end. They did not remain separate, and when the two joined with the more sober Roman culture, as happened in the British Isles of the seventh and eighth centuries, there was an explosion of missionary endeavour, scholarship, poetry and prayer which illuminated the so-called Dark Ages. The three primary colours had joined to form a rainbow.

Celtic spirituality

The faith of the Irish was centuries old by the time Augustine came to Thanet. It had matured and changed and begun to bring much to birth. But we have to accept that the 'Green Industry' has also distorted much of what we know of the Celtic saints. Many of the stories about them come from hagiographies written centuries after their death, of no historical significance at all except in that they tell us something of *the age in which they were written*. The pictures they give of ideas of sanctity two or three hundred years after the death of the early saints are interesting, and indeed appealing, but they are unlikely to reflect accurately the faith of the early Irish Christians.

John Macquarrie described the Celt as having 'an intense sense of presence . . . a God-intoxicated man whose life was embraced on all sides by the divine Being'. God was as real to them as their next-door neighbour and as close to them as their own heart. This produced a spirituality which was literally down to earth – established upon the creation and its goodness and yet everyday in its encompassing of the ordinary. How far is this true? There is evidence that there was a playfulness and a lightness of touch which we find appealing, but which some of their contemporaries might have found frivolous. Even as the monks beat back Satan by copying the Scriptures so they put in their illuminated letters miniatures of kittens playing and flowers blossoming. One of them even depicted mice nibbling the sacramental bread, a near-blasphemy which would never have occurred to the more sober-minded Romans.

There seems also to be little doubt that there was a overwhelming sense of the importance of the spiritual. But this is very far from the whimsy of some modern writing on the subject. The dreadful penitentials of Columbanus with their floggings and starvations for minor misdemeanours show that they took God seriously. There was no place for idleness or half-heartedness – or for fantasy or feyness.

The early Celtic saints were a good deal less 'politically correct' than they are sometimes portrayed today. However there is considerable evidence, not least in hagiographies and the poetry and other writings of the eighth and ninth centuries, that Celtic Christianity produced a spirituality which is particularly agreeable to twentieth-century people, both Christians and others. But we should not be anachronistic by reading back this spirituality into the age of Columba. One wonders what that warrior priest who led armies into battle would have made of those who have foisted upon him a spirituality of quiet acceptance which was so foreign to him. Similarly we have to beware of bestowing a unity of spirituality upon the eighth and ninth centuries. For example, the Culdees – eighth- and ninth-century Irish and Scottish hermits who banded together into communities of thirteen contemplatives – were violently misogynistic.

Hagiography

How historically accurate was this flowering of narratives of spirituality and learning and poetry? The people of that day said that the stories about the doings of the early British Christians and the wonders they performed were true. It was their way of claiming authority and was the literary convention of their day in the same way that Latin writers tended to attach to their own writings the name of one of their famous ancestors. The eighth- and ninth-century writers did not have the carefulness of Bede, who clearly sounds a cautionary note when he is unsure of the truth of a story. The claim that they were recounting historical fact seems to us to be nonsense, but their spirituality should be judged for itself, not dismissed because they held a different view of history to ourselves.

Standing between the early saints and this development of their Christianity a couple of hundred years later are two facts: the acceptance of Roman traditions and the Viking invasions. By 700 Roman ways were being grudgingly accepted. By 800 the Vikings had begun to arrive – just like the Anglo-Saxons before them, they came first in scattered raids and later they came to settle. The Celtic heartlands suffered as much as the better known invasions of England: Dalriada and the Scottish Isles were overrun, the Irish monasteries were put to the torch and sporadic warfare began. A contemporary tale begins ominously:

> There was a famous king here in Ireland, Ruadh son of Righdhonn of Munster. He had a meeting arranged with the Norwegians. He went to his meeting with the Norwegians round Scotland from the south, with three ships; there were thirty men in each ship.[1]

The scholarship and the poetry and the community died beneath the sword of the Viking. In holy Iona the monks were slaughtered, the sacred places defiled and buildings deserted.

But before that time and even during it there was a sweet flowering. It was during this time that many of the magnificent manuscripts were produced and scholarship abounded. It was also during this century that many of the hagiographies were written. A few of the early ones have some historical value: Stephanus wrote a *Life* of Wilfred in 720, only eleven years after the latter's death. Bede's *Lives of the Abbots of Wearmouth and Jarrow* was written shortly after the events it describes. By 800, however, the hagiographies had become almost pure fairy tale. The tales have a charm which comes from poetry not history.

But hagiography is important, not for historical evidence but as an insight into its own time. We can take the following story about St Brendan as an illustration. Brendan himself is speaking:

> One day when I was in this church, seven years ago to this very day, after preaching here and after Mass, the priests went to the refectory: I was left alone here, and a great longing for my Lord seized me, when I had gone up to the Body of Christ. As I was there, trembling and terror came upon me; I saw a shining bird at the window, and it sat on the altar. I was unable to look at it because of the rays which surrounded it, like those of the sun. 'A blessing upon you, and do you bless me, priest' it said. 'May God bless you' I said; 'who are you?' 'The angel Michael' it replied, 'come to speak to you . . . to bless you and to make music for you from your Lord' said the bird. The bird rubbed its beak on the side of its wing, and I was listening to it from that hour to the same hour next day; and then it bade me farewell.

That story can be taken at many levels. It may be a story of explanation. In the original setting Brendan is said to have 'had two balls of wax with a thread joining them' which he put in his ears whenever he heard music, for no music he heard later could match the beauty of the sound from the bird's wing. There may be a glimmer of history here: ear-plugs would have been useful for a scholar in a busy monastery, and it is possible Brendan used them. Certainly in the story Brendan takes the balls of wax from his ears to listen and 'put them on the book', which suggests that he was studying. Is the writer taking this very practical aid to study and giving it a more uplifting context?

But there is a spiritual truth which is independent of history.

Brendan is pictured as someone 'longing for my Lord', lingering in the church after the others had gone for their meal, quiet before the reserved sacrament, an experience of the Welsh word *liraeth* (yearning for God). And God met with him. It could be seen as merely an improving story to encourage monks to pray more before the sacrament, or, at a deeper level, an illustration of the biblical truth that 'those who seek after me shall find me'.

But there is also an aesthetic quality about the story. The shining of the bird and the beauty of the music are obvious, but also the literary quality of the whole story is clear. It begins with a student with a harp asking if he could play three tunes to Brendan. The monks explain about the balls of wax, but the student persists and eventually Brendan removes his ear-plugs and allows him to play. The story about the bird is given in reply to the student's natural question when the wax balls are replaced: 'Why do you not listen to the music? Is it because you think it bad?' The story ends with Brendan saying 'Take a blessing, student, and you shall have Heaven for that playing.' A well-constructed, coherent story.

There is only one detail which reminds us that we are in the eighth/ninth centuries. When the student first comes to the monks they say 'Brendan has been for seven years without smiling and without hearing any of the music of the world.' We would have liked a smile, for the closer presence of God surely brings great joy. And then a still deeper layer of the story suggests itself: who was the anonymous harpist? Could the angel Michael who appeared in the shape of a bird also come as a student?

These many-layered stories have a power of their own, for they are myths which say something of the spirituality of the eighth century, but we must not pretend that they say anything about the people they purport to speak about. The story above tells us nothing about Brendan himself, except the mere conjecture that he wore ear-plugs against the noise of the monastery.

From eighth-century spirituality to *Carmina Gadelica*

When, therefore, we say that much of the Celtic spirituality which is so popular today has no firm historical basis, we are only being partially accurate. It is unlikely that except in embryo it represents the actual spirituality of the first missionaries, but it does represent the full flowering of eighth-century spirituality. I have spoken half-jokingly about the 'Green Industry', which jumbles together material from a thousand years and puts it together into a new expression of faith. But there is something in it.

In the Western Isles of Scotland even to this day there is no Catholicism which is more orthodox and no Presbyterianism which is stricter in the whole wide world. Yet despite centuries of this conditioning an older and more personal spirituality still exists. All who study this stream of the Spirit are indebted to Alexander Carmichael who a century ago collected the customs and prayers of the ordinary people. They went to kirk or mass on Sunday but their folk religion was something very different from what they heard from the pulpits. One woman remembered how she was taught at home to start the day:

> My mother would be asking us to sing our morning song to God down in the back-house, as Mary's lark was singing it up in the clouds and as Christ's thrush was singing it yonder in the tree, giving glory to the God of the creatures for the repose of the night, for the light of the day and for the joy of life. She would tell us that every creature on the earth here below and in ocean beneath and in the air above was giving glory to the great God of the creatures and of the worlds, of the virtues and the blessings, and would we be dumb?[2]

It was from this rich source that there come the prayers which were said at certain times of the day or when doing certain tasks. Prayer was not something to be done only in church, but was part of the routine of kindling a fire, cutting the peat, shearing the sheep, milking the cows and so on.

Attractive as this material is, it is not to be accepted uncritically. There are superstitions and theology which need to be questioned. Ian Bradley describes a ritual which certainly does not have Christian roots, told him by the former parish priest of South Uist. There the custom was for a lump of fatty tissue to be taken from the breast of a newly killed sheep and hung on a rafter a few days before New Year. When it had dried out it was made into a kind of candle and carried around the house and then three times round the family gathered in the main room as a kind of blessing.[3]

It is sometimes said that the Celtic inheritance gathered by Carmichael and others is pantheistic, not distinguishing between the Creator and his creation. It certainly teeters on the brink at times, but, as in the example given above of the teaching given to Catherine Maclennan as a girl, the glory is given to God, not to the creatures who join their morning song in praise of the Creator – a theme straight from the Bible: 'O ye hills of the Lord, praise ye the Lord'.

The wonder is that with so little teaching to deepen and broaden this Celtic stream it remained so pure down so many centuries, so little affected by what went on at the Sunday services, whether Catholic or Protestant, which the people attended so assiduously.

It certainly touches a chord today. Books of Celtic prayers and Celtic sayings pour out. The theme is constant – that there was a golden age of spirituality which speaks to our age. I have argued above that the spirituality of the early saints is hidden from us by lack of evidence, but we are attracted to the spirituality (if poor history) of the eighth century and beyond.

Notes
1 Anonymous (eighth or ninth century).
2 Alexander Carmichael, *Carmina Gadelica*, 5 vols (1928–54).
3 Ian Bradley, *The Celtic Way* (1993).

Chapter 11

Conclusion

THE 'conversion' was a much more complex and significant event than is sometimes portrayed. It was not a matter of a few Italian monks coming to England, converting the kings and bringing into the full light of Rome the disobedient remnants of British Christianity.

Rather it is the weaving together of many stories. Some of them we know well for there is documentary and archaeological evidence. Others, especially from the Celtic side, are only hinted at, while still others are matters of conjecture. I have suggested that some parts of the 'Green Industry' have not done a service to this period of history because of a lack of historical integrity, for they have made the achievements of both Roman and Celtic missionaries the vehicle for particular spiritual and theological viewpoints. Certainly behind the clash between Roman and Celt there were profound differences of theology, attitude and practice. Many of these have modern resonances, but we do the early missionaries no favours by muddying the waters by importing our twentieth-century ideas.

After the conversion

As we have seen, the free-flowing, mobile, community-centred evangelism of the Celts was much more effective than the more leaden-footed Roman style. But it is the Roman organisation which we have inherited rather than a Celtic one. Is this just because of the power of Roman usage or does the Celtic style have the seeds of its own destruction within it? Is the Celtic pattern good for primary evangelism and poor at growing and continuing a church? Is a Celtic-style monastery inevitably going to decline in holiness and vigour?

The lessons of a book such as this can only be tentative, especially when seen as suggestions for modern practice. However, the following conclusions can be reached.

When a large group of people are not Christian, living in a society which has attitudes and an ethos which is not Christian, then the Celtic model of evangelism is more effective. Such evangelism needs to make room for the *peregrinati*: in modern terms these are the travelling evangelists and church-planters and the religious orders and places like Lee Abbey and Iona who are experimenting with small houses set in inner-city areas. Some work is being done by young people taking time off for a year or two to give to the work of God (though too easily they are sucked into a maintenance role within the system). These people need to be able to move and to breathe, to venture and take risks and learn from their mistakes.

After the 'conversion' of a nation or a community, when a 'Christendom' situation obtains, then *a settled Roman pattern is more satisfactory.* The regular work of the clergy in their closely confined areas in educating and influencing the community has had great impact for many centuries. However, for this to be fully effective, the majority of people must subscribe to the Christian faith, in theory if not in practice. There should be definable communities in which the Church has a recognisable place and in which the priest is a leader. This sense of community is dependent upon social factors as much as on density of population: there are many cities which are collections of villages, and villages where the sense of community has almost completely broken down.

Where there is a 'mixed economy' – where Christendom still has some vestiges of its former glory (and such communities still exist in many places) – *we need a mix of both Roman and Celtic forms of ministry.* We need the stability of the parish system, but we need also the freedom and ability to experiment of the entrepreneurial evangelist.

A 'mixed economy' is not easy. If we can jump 600 years forward from Anglo-Saxon England to the thirteenth century we see two forms of monastic order emerge. There were those derived from the static Benedictine pattern and there were those which had just sprung into existence as the Mendicant Orders. These were the very mobile friars, mainly Franciscan or Dominican. They operated in flat contradiction of Benedict's condemnation of the *gyrovagi*. They preached everywhere, begged for their daily bread and travelled without possessions in a lifestyle which is not unlike that of the early Celtic monks. In that comparatively prosperous period, they worked especially in the burgeoning new towns and cities which the existing parochial clergy were manifestly not touching. They went back to the Gospels and sought to imitate the life of Christ himself, a wanderer who relied on his Father for sustenance and who preached to all, outside the ecclesiastical machinery.

Initially the friars did not stir up much antagonism. They came directly under the authority of the Pope, and were free of obedience to any local bishop. They were also mainly lay – St Francis was lay most of his life and his successor was never ordained – and so did not come into conflict with other clergy. Their way of life was such that they were barely distinguishable from the many wild-eyed beggars and mountebanks which inhabited the streets of the towns of North Italy and France.

However they were enormously successful: they attracted many followers and in this lay the seeds of their own decline. They had a great reputation as confessors and in order that they might hear confessions 'officially' more and more members of the Mendicant Orders became priests, and so the Orders themselves were increasingly clericalised. They began to build churches with the gifts of the grateful, some of them still among the finest in Europe. In 1250 they obtained from the Pope permission to bury people in their own cemeteries, with an immediate effect on the remuneration of the local clergy. In 1281 Pope Martin IV allowed them to perform any pastoral function in any diocese or parish without the consent of the local bishops and priests, though this blanket permission to officiate was later reduced by later Popes.

The support the friars received from successive Popes during their formative period was remarkable. Indeed, it is one of the few examples of an institution allowing itself to be reformed from within, and accepting the tensions which this brings. Even if the Mendicant Orders lost their fire within a century and degenerated into the mischievous caricature given by Chaucer, they were a burning light which changed much and whose example still shines today.

We have to ask: who are the modern friars?

The 'New Evangelism'

I have identified what I call the 'New Evangelism'. This is by no means the creation of only the past few years, but there is no doubt that it is during that time that it has come to be the predominant force in British evangelism. As we have seen, the impetus behind it is a desire to explore and discover the being of God, a wish to walk alongside people in their exploration and a longing to make the Church and its doings helpful to them. Behind it is a passion for people that they should find the God who has meant so much to the 'New Evangelists'. This is not an easy form of evangelism – it is more costly than the older forms. In the more proclamatory methods of evangelism it is possible to stand away from people and preach the gospel *at* them. The 'New Evangelism' is more painful because it is more personal: it involves the evangelist in the whole life of the one who is coming to Christ. Nor is it any easier for a congregation, for it is much more demanding to maintain an attitude of care and welcome all the time, than to have a mission every five years.

A third element in this modern change of emphasis is the charismatic movement. I have included few examples of the miracles wrought by the early evangelists, because the evidence for them is often less than convincing. It is all too noticeable that the number of Bede's accounts of miracles increases the further they are from his personal experience. In those parts of contemporary history which he knew well, like the lives of the abbots he had known, the miraculous element is very limited.

But the Charismatic movement of our times is much more than a miracle-mongering sect, for it now comprises some 21 per cent of all Christians world-wide. Its emphases have a strongly Celtic flavour – it is more life-affirming and more ready to accept the role of the imagination than either traditional Catholicism or Protestantism; it believes in a God who works in the everyday lives of people; it expects God to act; it is prepared to experiment. In this it has caught the mood of the post-modern 1990s.

The opportunities for evangelism are great, for we live in a questing, unsettled age. The 'feel good' factor is noticeably absent, and with it the complacency which that engenders. Although it is only a date on the calendar, the approach of the third millennium provokes questions and visions. We live at a turning point and Christians have the opportunity to ensure that many people and communities find the living God.

Index

Aelle 11
Aethelfrith 18
Aetius 11
Agilberht 109f
Aidan viii, 5, 14, 18, 19, 30, 89n, 108, 128
Alaric the Goth 10
Alchfrith 109
Aldhelm 64, 110
Alfred, King 16, 57
Alphege 85
Alpha Courses 47
Anglo-Saxons, beliefs of 82f, 132; craftsmanship of 61; feasting by 84f, 89n; invasion by 8, ch. 1; kingdoms of 8, 12; kings ch. 7; language of 9, 12; love of violence of 99; myths of 81; poetry of 85; priesthood among 86; sacrifice among 84
Annegray 30, 57
Anthony of Egypt 52
Arthur, King 12, 94
atheism 44
Attila the Hun 9, 11
Augustine of Canterbury vii, viii, 2, 5, 8, 14, 23f, 26, 65, 97, 103ff, 115n, 118, 133
Augustine of Hippo 3, 22, 55, 81, 105, 107, 116, 119, 120ff, 124

Badonicus, Mons 12
Baldur 82, 83
Bamburgh 12, 30
Bangor 18
baptism 128

Basil 52
Bath 12, 96
Bede, the Venerable 6, 7, 8, ch. 2, 22, 25, 26, 53, 54, 61, 64, 103, 105, 109, 114n, 128, 135; *Ecclesiastical History* ch. 2; *On the Computation of Time* 17; *Lives of the Abbots* 136
'belonging and believing' 46f
Benedict 64; Rule of 63, 64f, 82, 106, 108, 111
Benedict Biscop 57, 61, 63, 73n, 115n
Benedictine monasteries 69
Bertha 23, 32n
Bible 7, 34, 61, 79, 107, 122, 124, 139
Birinus 32n, 108
bishops 5, 8, 54f, 58, 62, 93f, 104f, 109, 111f, 113f
Bobbio 31
Book of Kells 53, 61, 73; of Durrow 53, 60; Lismore 57
Bradbury 58
Breaking new Ground 70, 74n
Brendan 56, 136f
Brigit (Bridget) of Ireland 53f
Britannia, Roman province of 10
British 7, 22f; British Christians 8, 10, 103ff

Caedwalla 111
Caerwent 11
Candida Casa 27
Canterbury 2, 8, 24, 60, 65, 112
Carmina Gadelica 137f
Cassiodorus 61
Catholicism, Roman 20, 38, 43
Cedd 30, 58, 109

Celtic Christianity viii, 4, 26f, 122ff; 132f; churches and Byzantium 116f; crosses 116; discipline and prayer 68; evangelism viii, 2, 28, 31; knot 27, 126f; literature 60; manuscripts 53, 61; mission to the English 26, 31; monasticism 23, 53ff, 67ff; monastic mission of ch. 5; peoples in East and West 116f; preaching 126ff; saints viii, 4, 6, 8; scholarship 53; sense of adventure 71; spirituality viii, 3, 6, 51, 133f, 137f; theology 118f, 122ff

Celts and Romans contrasted viii, 2, 6, 18f, 47f, 55, 60, 105f, 112, 116f, 118, 126, 140f

Cenwalh of Sussex 18

Cerdic 12

Chad 30

Charismatic movement 3, 43, 143f

Chelsea, Council of 107

Christendom vii, 1f, 2, 79f, 80f, 93

Christians for Life 47

Church as living community 45; marginalised in today's society 80

church-planting 28, 58, 66f, 69f, 74n

church structures, Roman and Celtic 5, 56, 106, 112f

circle prayers 88, 125f

Codex Amiatinus 62

Coifi 25, 85

Colman 109f, 118

Columba viii, 2, 14, 19, 28f, 67, 134f

Columbanus 23, 30f, 33n, 58f, 62, 67, 105; rule of 62, 65, 134

Columbanian communities 57, 65, 69

comitatus (warband) 94

community, monastic 67

Constantine 11

conversion, of England vii, 7, 140; sudden or gradual 40

Cornwall 7, 8, 13, 14, 57, 67

Coroticus 4

Cunedda 14

Cuthbert of Lindisfarne 5f, 18, 19, 64, 108

Dagan 107

Dalriada 14, 29, 135

'Damascus Road' 40f

Decade of Evangelism viii, 2, 37f, 48n

Deorham, battle of 12

doctrine to spirituality, from 42f

Dorchester 32

Dream of the Rood 83

druidic religion 4, 5, 132f

Dyfed dynasty 14

Eaconberht, King 92

Easter, dating of 55, 94, 106, 111, 128

Eastern churches 21, 22, 107, 115n, 116, 119

Ecgrith, King 18, 93

education, Celtic, Roman and Saxon 60

Edmund 85

education, evangelism by 72; in monasteries 72

Edwin, King of Northumbria 24, 29, 85, 92, 109

Egypt 51, 54

'Emmaus, road to' 40ff

England, evangelisation of vii, ch. 3, 118

English, the 7

Enlightenment, the 34, 36, 75, 76, 88n

Ethelbert, King of Kent 23f, 32n, 97

ethical questions 36, 79, 80

evangelisation of England, from Rome ch. 3; from Celtic churches 30f; place of king in ch. 7; and social change 99f

evangelism, Celtic compared with Roman 2, 39ff, 47f, 56, 112f, 141; from event-centred to pastoral 47; the 'New' viii, ch. 4 (esp. 38f, 45ff), 130, 143; criticisms of the 'New' 48; in the public realm 72f

experience, spiritual (in ordinary life) 43

faith, modern journey of 46; community of 78f

Finding Faith Today 45, 46, 49

Fontaine 57

Formosus, Pope 87

Francis of Assisi 33n, 142

Franks Casket 81

Fursey 31

Gaul 21, 23, 26, 31, 52f, 57, 59, 104, 105, 116, 123

Gildas 8, 11, 12, 103, 114n

Gloucester 11

'Gospel, and Our Culture' movement 73, 75

Goths 10, 21
Graham, Billy 23, 38, 39, 41
'Green Industry' viii, 3, 119, 134, 138, 140
Gregory I (the Great), Pope 21ff, 31, 53, 55, 64, 97, 100, 103f, 105, 112, 115, 117, 118, 129f
gyrovagi ('gadabouts') 65, 70

hagiography viii, 135ff
'Have Another Look' 39
heaven 99
hell 99, 123
hermits 51f
Hertford, Synod of 58, 110, 114
Hilary of Arles 55
Hilary of Poitiers 52
Hilda of Whitby 59, 109
holiness 5; holy places 6
Honorius (emperor) 11
Honorius I (Pope) 32n, 108
Huns 9f

identity, search for 44
Ine, King of Wessex 92
INFORM 42, 88n
Iona 3, 6, 26, 29, 30, 54f, 67, 110, 111, 136
Ireland 4, 6, 14, 21, 26, 27f, 53ff, 97, 117
Irish, the 7, 18, 20, 22; mission to England 26ff, 31, 67f; 'wanderers' 57
Islam 1, 36, 80f
Ithamar 26

James the Deacon 109
Jarrow 6, 62
Jerome 52, 120f
JIM (Jesus In Me) 39
John IV, Pope 108
John Scotus Erigena 123f, 125
Justinian 64, 117
Jutes 10

Kenneth McAlpin 14
kingship ch. 7; and deity 98

Lastingham 58
Lawrence of Canterbury 24, 107f
Lay initiatives 68
Lichfield 30
Lincoln 25

Lindisfarne 2, 6, 26, 30, 58, 108
liturgy, Roman and Celtic 105f
Llantwit Major 60
Loire Valley 54
Loki 34, 83
London 32, 112
Luidhard, Bishop 32n
Luxueil 58

Manichaeanism 121, 124f
Martin of Tours 18, 27, 52, 54, 117
mega-culture 75f
Mellitus of London 112
Mendicant orders 142
Mercia 8, 12
meta-narratives 36
midi-cultures 76f
mini-cultures 78
ministers 113f
'Minus to Plus' 39
mission, theology of ch. 9 (esp. 118ff); and movement 66
missions to mission, from 45f
modernism 34, 75
monasteries 28; as centres of mission ch. 5; 'monastery-planting' 28, 66; double 59f, 83
monasticism, beginnings of 51ff
Mons Badonicus 12
Monte Cassino 64

National Lottery 66, 80
Nennius 19
New Age 1, 35, 36, 76
'New Religious Movement' (NRMs) 1, 42
Ninian (Nynia) 5, 19, 27
Norman Conquest 163
Northumbria 6, 8, 12, 19, 25, 26, 29, 30, 57

'On Fire' 39
'Operation Mobilization' 71
Orosius 11
Oswald 29f, 132
Oswiu, king 94, 107, 109f, 130

Pachomius 52, 53
Palau, Luis 38
Palladius 27, 122
parish system 5, 114
Patrick 4, 27f, 33n, 54, 127

Paulinus viii, 14, 19, 25, 26, 29, 100, 112
Pelagianism 107, 108, 117, 119ff, 123f
Pelagius 107, 117, 119ff, 131n
Penda, king of Mercia 25, 30, 58, 132
peregrinati ('wanderers') 56, 65
perichoresis 126
Pevensey (Anderida) 12
Picts 14, 18, 20, 29
Poland 31, 57
pope/s, the 6, 27, 94, 100f, 107, 110, 142
post-modernism 34f, 36f, 45, 75, 80
predestination 124
Protestantism 4, 6, 20, 43, 143

Raedwald, King of the East Angles 83, 96
relationships 46
Rhine 10
Ripon 65
Rochester 24, 26
Romania 10, 31, 116
Roman civilisation 96f; Empire 10f, 21, (revival of Empire) 22, 97
Rome, Church of vii, 6, 28, 116f; mission to Anglo-Saxon England 6, ch. 3; style of church organisation 5, 32
Rome, city of 10, 21f, 57, 122

St Albans 11
St Gall 31
'St Patrick's Breastplate' 88
St Paul's Cathedral, London (the first) 24
Saints Alive! 47
Scotland 7, 8, 13, 14, 21, 25, 27, 29, 54, 55, 118, 135
Scotti 7, 15
self-awareness 44; -fulfilment 44
Sigebert, king 24, 95, 98
Signs of Life 39
sin, original 121; sense of 43, 130
soul friend (Celtic) 133
spiritual experience 43; journey 41; search 44
Sussex 11

Sutton Hoo 13, 60f, 96
syncellus 133
Syria 51, 54, 74

Taizé 3
Taranto 31
Thanet 23
Theodore of Tarsus 5, 60, 100, 110, 114, 115n
Third Order 68, 74n
Thor 34, 82
Tilbury 58
Tobias of Rochester 60
today 1f, 3f, 5, ch. 4, 73, 75–81, 87, 100–102, 130, 141ff
tonsure, Eastern/Celtic and Roman 106, 115n
tributum 112, 113
Trinity, the Holy 126
Turnbull Commission 37

'uncertainty principle' 34

Valhalla 85
Vandals 122f
Vikings 11, 50, 61, 64, 99, 114, 135
Vortigern 10

Waldemar I, King of Denmark 91
Wales 7, 8, 13, 14, 21, 26, 54, 55, 60, 104
Wallsend 6, 16
Welsh, the 7, 17, 19, 31, 60, 104, 110
Wessex 8, 12
Whitby, Synod of viii, 6, 20, 55, 94, 103, 104, 107, 108ff, 115n, 118, 130
Whithorn 27, 29, 33n
Wilfred 25, 65, 93, 108ff, 111, 136
Winchester 13
Woden (Odin) 82, 93, 132
women, attitudes to 59, 121
Worcester 65
writing, Anglo-Saxon knowledge of 86
wyrd 83f

Yeavering 12, 84
York 12, 23, 25, 112